7/01

A DEEPER FREEDOM

A DEEPER FREEDOM

Liberal Democracy as an Everyday Morality

CHARLES W. ANDERSON

THE UNIVERSITY OF WISCONSIN PRESS

The University of Wisconsin Press
1930 Monroe Street
Madison, Wisconsin 53711

www.wisc.edu/wisconsinpress/

3 Henrietta Street
London WC2E 8LU, England

1   3   5   4   2

Printed in the United States of America

Library of Congress Cataloging-in-Publication Data

Anderson, Charles W., 1934-
A deeper freedom: liberal democracy as
an everyday morality / Charles W. Anderson.
220 pp.   cm.
Includes bibliographical references and index.
ISBN 0-299-17610-X (cloth: alk. paper)
1. Democracy—Moral and ethical aspects.
2. Liberalism—Moral and ethical aspects.
3. Social ethics.   I. Title.
JC423 .A537   2002
321.8—dc21   2001005412

CONTENTS

Acknowledgments   vii
Introduction   ix

Part I   Philosophy

1   A Dialogue between Generations   3
2   The Awakening and the Meaning of It All   11
3   Living Philosophically and Living Well   22

Part II   Individuality

4   What Is Freedom For?   35
5   Individuals and the Powers Within   54
6   On Human Frailty and the Problem of Evil   76

Part III   Relationships

7   Individuality and Relationship   93
8   Teaching and Learning   109
9   Community   133
10   Working Relationships   148
11   Democracy   170

Part IV   Humanity

12   Who Do We Think We Are?   185

Notes   201
Index   206

ACKNOWLEDGMENTS

I am grateful to four trusted friends who commented on the manuscript. Booth Fowler, Adolf Gundersen, Thomas Spragens, and Suzanne Duval Jacobitti gave me careful, helpful advice and encouragement, and with Suzanne this led to one of the most intense and probing philosophic discussions of my life. I am also grateful for the helpful comments of an anonymous reviewer for the University of Wisconsin Press.

The thoughts from which I fashioned this book developed throughout a lifetime of teaching, mainly at the University of Wisconsin–Madison and most recently at the University of West Florida. I thank all those students and colleagues who inspired me, perplexed me, and told me how things seemed from their own angle of vision. I must single three out, for what they taught me influenced this book directly and specifically. Juliana Hunt knows precisely the sentence she wrote that fixed my mind on the haunting fact of individuality. Ruth Lessl Shively calmly, politely, but with relentless reason showed me what it meant to be absolutely serious about the problem of truth. And Adolf Gundersen, again, taught me new implications and possibilities in the Socratic dialogue.

My literary models are four nature writers who, starting from their academic specialties, used the essay form to express a larger vision of amazement at the world. These are Annie Dillard (literature), Loren Eiseley (paleontology), Aldo Leopold (wildlife management), and Lewis Thomas (microbiology). I wanted to see whether I could do the same for my disciplines of political theory and political economy. This is the result.

I am grateful once again to the people at the University of Wisconsin Press for their usual care and skill in the production of this book.

Finally, and as always, I am grateful to Jeanie for a relationship that, through everything, seems constantly to grow in wonder and discovery.

INTRODUCTION

To live successfully we need both a public and a personal philosophy, and the two must mesh. To assemble the ideals and ideas that will guide our lives, we necessarily draw on the beliefs and understandings of a particular people, how they imagine things to be.

Thus arises the great responsibility of the people of a democracy. It is one that is seldom discussed. But the fact of the matter is that when the people debate the principles that will guide their public life, as they must, they must ask also what they intend individuals to draw from these ideals as they try to give purpose and meaning to their lives.

We tend to think of a cultural legacy as an unconscious tradition, something we pass on by instinct from generation to generation. But our public philosophy, liberal democracy, is a conscious contrivance. It is something that we have created and decided. It is also something we continue to argue, interpret, and refine. Thus it is in order for us to ask reflectively and continuously just what philosophy—what view of the human situation and human purpose—we intend to pass on to the next generation.

Public philosophy is not just concerned with the functions of government. It is also the source of our reflections on ourselves, our understanding of the nature of things, the significance of our presence here, and right and wrong. In the end the most important question that a free people must ask itself is simply, "What should we teach the children?"

This is a book about the political ideals of individual freedom and democracy. But mainly this book is about individuality and relationships. Many today believe that the public philosophy of liberal democracy cannot serve as the basis of a personal ethic. They think that to teach individual freedom leads only to self-seeking and permissiveness and that the young must be taught a counterethic of duty and obedience to established ways. Others, mainly in the academy, believe that individual freedom is an illusion, that society determines and socially situates the self.

For some the very idea of individual freedom has come to sound false and hollow, for it is used so often and so loudly by the self-seeking and the sullen, those who think the main aim of life should be personal aggrandizement and those who are so fearful and mistrustful that they seek only to separate themselves in gated suburbs or militia compounds.

I look for the precise sense in which the life of individual freedom can be a worthy way of life. I start from the simple fact that each individual is unique. Though much is said these days about diversity and difference, this seems to mean mainly group differences, specifically those of race, class, and gender, and not those astonishing differences that arise from the fact that each individual is a particular bundle of temperament and talent, frailty and temptation.

I go on to explore the ways in which we reach out to find one another, to form free relationships, not socially constructed but fashioned by ourselves, as we seek through love and inquiry to understand one another and create common ground.

From there I build up to the great themes of education, economics, and politics, community, markets, and democracy. And I do this against the background of our shared sense of surprise that there should be creatures like us at all, all of one kind yet each distinct, constantly in wonder at the world, and constantly trying to figure out what we were put here for, what we were intended to do.

Who is this "we" that I invoke throughout? It is everyone and anyone who believes in individual freedom as a crucial value of personal and public life, all those who are properly called "liberal" in the classic sense, though some may prefer other terms for their political identity. I speak of this collective "we" to suggest a collective deliberation among all those who seek a deeper freedom.

PART I

Philosophy

1

A Dialogue between Generations

Every generation must provide a legacy to the next. The elders school the young in their ways, in their conceptions of what is worthy and what is not, where meaning lies, the distinction between right and wrong, the genuine and the counterfeit. The young, for their part, assess their legacy. Some teachings they sustain. Some they disavow. Others they simply neglect.

Some elders, of course, are themselves rebels. They teach against established ways. And some of the young are zealous traditionalists. Nonetheless, in general the fate of the elders is to be the conservators. They would reproduce themselves, biologically and philosophically. Have any parents ever wanted their children to repudiate their values? Similarly, the young must necessarily assess their inheritance. It does not determine them; they have free will.

The process is innate and instinctive. It is perhaps the most elementally human thing that we do. The old must instruct the young. It is their duty, for the young must have language and knowledge, technique and meaning. The young in turn must ponder and appraise. They must interpret, improve, reject, and deny. Close up, this is the tale of love and hurt, closeness and estrangement, in every family. In the large, it is the story of continuity and revolution, vitality and decline, in every civilization.

Today we are most uneasy about this whole matter. Many elders are unsure what to teach. Many young people themselves are cautious and bewildered, unsure about what they are willing to

3

receive, though they urgently want to receive something. After a long third of a century of questioning all conventions, all mores, all patterns of authority, both sides of the generational dialogue are wary. The political, sexual, and ethical turmoil of our times has shattered our confidence. We do not know how to carry on the natural, inevitable process of passing on a lesson. This might seem to be the worst of times to consciously discuss our philosophical and ethical commitments. But it might also be the best of times. We all know there are no obvious answers. Right now we might be able to honestly take stock.

What indeed ought we to teach? What are the hard, sure convictions that we most urgently want to perpetuate? What ideas and values are we convinced that the next generation must embrace if they are to lead good lives? What ideas must they spurn if they are not to be ruined?

We have a history, but we are no longer sure that we know what story it is to tell. Is it to be a tale of human challenge and adventure, opportunity and achievement, or one of the plunder of a continent and the oppression of its peoples?

We have a language (perhaps languages) and a way with numbers to teach. But what other skills should all the young possess? Given the complexities of our technology, which should we take to represent the common stock of practical knowledge? Need all know how to sow and reap? Need all know the intricacies of the financial markets, our finely tuned methods of avarice? Should all know how the Internet works? How about household plumbing?

We have a heritage of literature, art, and scientific understanding. How much of this should be part of the common culture? Remember, please, that the young do not have time for everything. What are our priorities?

But the hardest questions concern our deepest values and beliefs, our understandings of the meaning of life, where we stand on love and hate, where we draw the line between tolerance and evil. We recognize that these are the most urgent questions. We recognize also that here we are on the shakiest ground. These are, we say, intimate and private matters. We do not decide them in public. They are to be settled in the bosom of the family and ultimately in the mind of the individual. Of that much we are very certain. Here, at least, we seem to be on common ground.

Very well. Let us affirm together that no one can legislate ultimate beliefs. We must choose them freely. But is this one firm affirmation all that we intend to say? Are we, the elders, simply not going to discuss truth and love and good and evil and meaning? Is it improper for us to consciously consider what we want to say, as a people, about these matters? Do we really think that the fundamental beliefs of the next generation should arise randomly from whatever falls out from the whole stream of chatter, fashion, merchandising, proselytizing, all the accidental trivialities of an age? Do we want the answers to the most important questions to just happen? Are we naïve enough to think that the truth will always prevail? Or are we simply tongue tied and hamstrung, so intimidated by all the ways we have been taught that it is possible always to think otherwise that we feel unable to utter a single truth?

Clearly, we have to teach the principles of liberal democracy. This commitment is strongly shared. We are, curiously, a philosophical republic, the nation that, as Mr. Lincoln put it, was founded on a proposition.

The ideal of individual freedom, said to be "self-evident," is the centerpiece of this public philosophy. But it is inherently contentious. Indeed, the world has argued about little else these past three or four hundred years. How, then, do we intend to construe individual freedom as we prepare the next generation to search out life's meanings?

Certainly, we do not believe that a person can live well in docile conformity and submission. Life cannot simply be about carrying out the mandates of others. Somehow, we feel, life must be a conscious work, an intentional creation, and for this to be possible, individuals must be free to act on their own responsibility.

But do we not also believe that a society that commits itself to personal freedom, *and nothing more than that,* is apt to become a society of self-seeking and self-indulgence, a society in which personal gratification becomes the only goal? Such a society, we suspect, is far from neutral about life's possibilities. Is not a society committed only to personal freedom likely to promote and celebrate envy and contempt, success won through friendless ambition, loveless eroticism, loneliness, carelessness?

Some would affirm individual freedom as the foundation of the public philosophy simply on the ground of skepticism. They doubt that any individual or elite can presume to know surely life's meaning and purpose. Thus all are entitled to live as they choose.

However, there is an idea of individual freedom that is deeper and fuller. That is the one that I want to explore here. I want to examine in detail our capacity for self-consciousness and self-awareness, the strange power within us to penetrate appearances and conventions; to interpret, criticize, and pass judgment on the teachings of the elders; and in the end to ask whether their strictures are worthy as they stand or need improvement.

I want to explore this idea of human capabilities that underlies and gives significance to the principle of individual freedom. In the next chapter I start at the beginning. I want to go back to what we presume were our first moments of wakefulness, to the time when we seem first to have become aware that something was peculiar about the world and our presence in it, something that required explanation. I want to show how our philosophy or religion, all our collective thought, has grown out of this strange awareness of ourselves. I will stress—for many think individuality is only a modern idea—how from the first moments of Greek, Jewish, Christian, and Roman thought we have been aware of the distinctiveness of minds, that each person partakes in a particular way in the universal capacity to wonder, to inquire, to try to understand. Arguably, other of the world's great religious and philosophic traditions have taught the same. I go into all this, albeit briefly, because I want to make clear how deep and significant the ideas of individuality and freedom actually are.

I then ask what it would mean to live philosophically, which is to say, self-consciously and thoughtfully. I hope to show that this way of life is ordinary, not exalted, though only some—we have no idea how many—achieve it.

I shall go on to ask, quite bluntly, what we intend to teach the members of the next generation about their individuality, their freedom, and their bonds to one another. What do we want to tell them about why we value freedom, what do we mean when we say that we want them to develop the best that is in them? How are they to understand their capacity for good and evil?

Then I take up the question of how we can reach out from our solitude and find one another to establish relationships and communities. Here I dwell on the idea of inquiry—that, given our incompleteness, we can only know through the others, that only in relationship can we begin to understand.

This process of seeking one another, of questing and discovery, of criticism and correction that is inquiry, is how we find one another at all levels of life—in friendship, love, work, and politics. Inquiry is the method of human understanding that is common to the Socratic dialogue, Aristotelian practical reason, scientific investigation, and liberal democratic deliberation.

I want, then, to teach a fuller, more classic view of humanity and the significance of individuality and freedom as the foundation of an understanding of liberal democracy that we might pass along. This view of how we might best represent ourselves to ourselves has its origins in the teachings of Plato and Aristotle, Jesus of Nazareth, the Roman Stoics, St. Augustine and St. Thomas, Kant and Hegel, and, most proximately, Charles Sanders Peirce and John Dewey. This is the view that underlies much of our tradition. It takes seriously the human capacity to transcend culture and does not try to explain it away.

I am interested in the human qualities that make us capable of wonderment and dissatisfaction and of critical and practical reason. We are the creatures who have the ability to seek excellence and efficiency in the moral sense, which means fittedness to purpose. These are powers as mysterious as they are commonplace. We are creatures who are clearly capable of asking about the point of our endeavors and then pressing the question beyond immediate, instrumental goals until we come to a notion of our essential aim, which then becomes a moral quality, a conception of what we should do. We are the ones who can measure our performance against an idea of final function, of telos, or of form that exists nowhere in our tangible experience but only in our minds.

We do this everyday, all the time. It is among the most natural of our activities. The thought guides the form. Through it we create the artifact.

We learn the skills and practices, methods and graces of our culture. But we do not simply conform to a teaching. We also work to polish and perfect these skills. We want to use them well, harmoniously, judiciously, precisely. This is also part of the human propensity that interests me. Even our desire to copy an exemplar exactly (a swimming stroke, the accent of another language, a song) involves our strange sense for corrigibility, our ability to recognize a disparity between our action and the model, and our ability then to try to duplicate the model, to capture its very spirit. Often, we have no exemplar. We seek intuitively to get in touch with the spirit of a situation, to find the flow.

But we also tend to make personal interpretations. And we are capable of challenging our culture's norms, measuring them against ideal notions that we discern vaguely within. We are capable of asking of a technique, "Is this the best we can do?" Or of a law, "Is this really fair?" We cannot point to our referent. We do not know it from philosophy or history. We can say that we do not live in a perfect community, though we have no experience that would enable us to say what such a community would be like.

I want to argue this classic view of humanity, of individuality, community, and freedom, against three specific contending positions. I chose these three alternatives because I think they are the most influential of the self-images of the age. They permeate our consciousness. We teach them, intentionally, deliberately, to the young. I want to show that none of these representations of the human situation is necessary or inevitable. We are not required to endorse them.

The first of these contending views is the spare utilitarian doctrine that sees the individual as calculating egoist and freedom as the persistent quest for satisfaction. This view teaches that seeing life's purposes as a sum of benefits is natural and that we live well if we constantly weigh and calculate our actions, seeking just that path that will maximize our utility and minimize our displeasure. Many call this is an objective doctrine, impartial among ideas of human purpose and the human good. But this view is no more neutral about human nature and human possibilities than any other. It teaches a very specific idea of human aims and human reason and what human beings are supposed to do.

The second position that I wish to dispute might be called cultural conservatism. It is a common form of contemporary relativism. This is the view that the self is no more than a social construct. We are a reflection of some image of humanity of our time and place. We would be otherwise had we been born elsewhere or in a different age. Individual freedom, our very ability to act with purpose, is a product of the social roles, the images and understandings, that our culture provides. The source of our vague yearnings—for beauty, for justice—lies in nothing universal, nothing within. These yearnings are instead intimations grounded in traditions, contingent social products that people of a different place or past may not be able to grasp at all.

The third position that I would contest is generally called postmodernism. In its relativism it is in some ways related to cultural conservatism. Essentially, this is the teaching that when we finally become fully aware of the contingency of our thought, of its quality as a human artifact, we will recognize that it is not binding on us, and we can then become truly free, unbound by any strictures. We will understand the cunning of reason—that it gives power to some and subordinates others. Seeing this, we can be free to face the meaninglessness of the world squarely and joyfully. This is, of course, the teaching of those who follow in the tradition from Friedrich Nietzsche.

Of course, we are the creators of our conceptions of ourselves. How could it be otherwise? Other animals are told their nature. But we are the creatures who must define our purposes and meaning and thus our fate.

The tendency of the times is to trivialize this capacity for self-definition, to treat it disdainfully, ironically. Many images of the self, of the human situation, exist. Dismissing them all as equally arbitrary "social constructions," the products of our pretensions and of our whimsy, is easy. We are taught that evaluating these visions, ascertaining which might come closer to our actual nature, is impossible. Those that succeed, that define an epoch or a civilization, are not necessarily closer to the truth. No, these are just the ideas that happen to catch on.

I do not believe that we should take so lightly the creation of these images of humanity. Rather, I think that this is the most important work that we do and that it calls for all our seriousness and all our subtlety. After all, we cannot suppose just anything about ourselves. We are a phenomenon in nature. We have characteristics that can be observed. We can then scrutinize these qualities, examine them in full awareness of all that we can recognize about our selves, the ways that we are like, and the ways that we are different from, other phenomena of nature. We can ask which conceptions of our situation better capture what we seem to be.

The most important task in this work of self-definition is the creation of the public philosophy. The public philosophy is the practical expression of all our conjecture. The public philosophy does not have to do with the order of the state alone. Rather, it is the deliberate part of our conception of the human situation and human purpose. It is what we think we should commonly suppose about our nature and our destiny. In the end the crucial function of the public philosophy is as a foundation for education. This is the understanding of ourselves that we wish to perpetuate, that we will to pass along.

The temper of this book is one of inquiry. The form is more that of dialogue than argument. My aim is not to use evidence or logic to refute the contending views. Rather, I ask whether one form of self-understanding better fits our common intuitions of who we are and what we were intended to do.

Should we expect to reach consensus? Perhaps. Perhaps not. Much depends on the integrity that we bring to the engagement. But to the extent that we differ, we will at least be aware of why we differ. And because inquiry is unending, we can then go on to ask how we shall define our relationship and our teaching in the light of our differences. That much is inherent in the idea of inquiry. That much is a necessary part of liberal democratic politics.

2

The Awakening and
the Meaning of It All

We are the inheritors of a specific vision of humanity, public and personal, that we call liberal democracy. But this system of beliefs, this philosophy, is set in a larger background of rumination and faith. What, then, did the elders tell us that made us conscious of the possibility of individual freedom? How did we come to suppose that we were not just members of the tribe but that we had the power within us to examine the legacy that we had received and to ask whether we could make it better? How did we first become aware of the strangeness of the world, that we live in mystery?

We imagine that our distant ancestors, sitting by their cave fires, must have wondered too. But we do not know this. We are simply supposing that humans have always felt the need to unravel the mystery of their presence on this planet. But they left no record. They did not speak to us.

But perhaps they did not wonder at all. Perhaps the miracle of the emergence of mind is even greater than we might suppose. Perhaps this strange capacity of our kind arose (or was implanted?) quite suddenly, at a time in the history of the earth incredibly close to our own. Perhaps we are really very new, astonishingly inexperienced, at this sort of thing.

What the record actually suggests is that at some recent point in evolutionary history, say, between twenty-five hundred and three thousand years ago, a few people became aware. The probing questioning, the search for a reality that lies beneath the surface,

11

began with strange simultaneity in different parts of the world. The development of Greek philosophy, the creation of the holy texts of Judaism, the teachings of Guatama Buddha and of Confucius all occur within a very compressed period. The crucial moment lies roughly between 900 and 350 B.C.E.[1]

We believe that hominids, beings like us, have walked the earth for a little less than four million of the earth's five billion years. But long eras passed before they seemed to do much more than chip stone. Perhaps 40,000 years ago we began to make traps and spears, construct hearths and shelters. Between 10,000 and 25,000 years ago art appeared, then agriculture, permanent settlement. Writing came later.

A remarkable quickening in human evolution occurs quite recently. We do not yet comprehend its significance. But the entire venture of philosophy, science, and religion to which we are party is a matter of the last few moments of evolutionary time. Could this mean that we are far closer to the beginning than the end of our quest?

I like to imagine that we, as humanity, became awake and aware with a start, quite suddenly, as we as individuals sometimes become awake and aware with a start, quite suddenly.

And I like to think that when we awoke, dazed and bedazzled, we asked three primary questions, which are probably the only questions worth asking. These questions have guided all our inquiry, all our puzzlement and wonder, ever since.

The first question would have been, "Where are we?" We have arrived in the middle of a show that has quite obviously been going on for some time, and we do not know the plot and the action. We have arrived on the scene without explanation, and we do not recognize or comprehend our whereabouts. What is more, by some uncanny sixth sense we suspect that more is going on here than meets the eye. We call our efforts to answer this first primary question science and theology and, if you will, metaphysics and ontology.

The second primary question would have been, "Who are we?" We are obviously a creature in nature, and other creatures are around, alive, abundant, curiously diverse. But what are we to make of the fact that there are creatures ask such questions as we do? Why should there be creatures like this at all? So we create images of human nature, and we call these efforts psychology, and sometimes poetry and religion and perhaps epistemology, for we are the creatures that seek to know, so we need a theory of knowledge and the knowable.

And then most fatefully, we would have asked, "And what are we expected to do?" In that moment, with this extraordinary question, we reveal our nature, and then we must go on to create a politics and an economics and an ethics.

The particular strand in this quest that underlies our inheritance of thought and conjecture began, we believe, in the vicinity of Miletus on the Aegean Sea (in present-day Turkey), somewhere around 600 B.C.E.

The apparent transience and contingency of nature impressed the Greeks. Everything, they realized, could have been different. What, then, is permanent and enduring? This led them to ask about the underlying nature of reality, what was real despite appearances, what was lasting in a world of flux. Thales, reflecting on the four elements that were basic to the Greeks—earth, air, fire, and water—proposed water as the lasting element, for it seemed to him part of all else, and it could take the form of a solid, a liquid, or a gas. In time the discussion deepened. Democritus proposed the existence of a fundamental particle, different and more basic than the visible elements of this world, out of which everything is composed. Thus was born atomism and materialism and a quest to reduce all reality to the hard stuff of the world that continues today. But Heraclitus proposed a radically different answer. Perhaps the true basis of reality was not matter but mind, an ordering idea that was eternal and unchanging and that gave form, character, and destiny to all the elements of the existing world. Thus was born idealism, and our ruminations on the mystery of the universe and our place within it have never been quite the same. Pythagoras, Plato, and Aristotle followed this thread of supposition and found remarkable implications in it. The guiding of our minds by mathematical logic and abstract ideals seemed more than an accident to them. They put forth the daring thought that in certain of its explorations, the mind could touch at least the edge of the deeper forms that gave order to the universe.

But many strongly disagreed with Pythagoras, Plato, and Aristotle. Many doubted that the mind could penetrate beneath surface features, the substantial world, and our ordinary ways of knowing it. Protagoras and the Sophists were suspicious. Probably, they taught, we can know no more than the evidence of our senses and the workings of our minds. Others carried on the materialist tradition and supplied it with an ethic. The Epicureans taught that all experience, ultimately, was pleasure and pain, satisfaction and dissatisfaction, and thus the problem was to live as well as possible guided by this realization of the limits of our understanding. Their lineal descendants include the modern utilitarian economists. To a remarkable extent these long ruminations of twenty-five hundred years ago frame the way we have thought about the most important problems ever since.

All the reasonings and insights, the discoveries, narratives, and findings, that follow from these first propositions are what we have to work with. These are the foundation questions behind our philosophy, our science, and our religion. This is the basis of our legacy. The problem now is what we want to make of it, how we want to represent it.

We often describe the history of our philosophy as disputatious and inconclusive. Perhaps this is because we examine it too closely. We have been taught to distinguish all the schools. Plato thought this. Aristotle thought that. Immanuel Kant, Georg Wilhelm Friedrich Hegel, and David Hume thought something else again. Thus we miss the remarkable continuities in all these teachings. To an extraordinary extent all the great thinkers of the West, and of the East too, have given strikingly similar answers to the most important questions.

In fact, no important philosophy or religion has ever taught that it understood the whole truth about the nature of the world or the intentions of God. What all the great philosophies and religions teach is the distance between our best speculations and the actual nature of ultimate reality. Yet they also all stress the strange, uncanny fact that we are creatures who can recognize that we do not know it all. How in the world is this possible? How can the fallible suspect truth? How can the finite suppose infinity? At the end of our most daring speculations and visions is enchanted bewilderment. At the end of it all we really do not know where we are, or who we are, or what we are expected to do. We really have no idea of why we are in the world or why the world exists at all.

Socrates made a special point of proclaiming his ignorance. Plato, surely the most daring of them all, taught that if we went about it properly we would see that all our ideas and judgments culminate in a vague sense of a perfect ideal, a form of justice perhaps or harmony or beauty. But Plato did not teach that either he or Socrates had achieved true knowledge of the forms, and he certainly did not think that a group of philosophers, through intense dialectic, would achieve this knowledge and go on to create a perfect political order.

We are fated to live in the cave. But what is interesting is that we are capable of seeing the point of the allegory. We actually can suspect that the cave is not our real home.

Nor did Aristotle think that we were going to find final answers. But he produced fascinating practical methods for wringing more meaning out of the appearances by asking questions about what we take to lie behind the appearances: What are our real, our final, purposes? What do we take to be the essential nature of a thing? What is a phenomenon, an object, a being, an idea tending toward? What would it become if it lost all contingency, all imperfection?

Christians through all ages have taught that we can only come to understand our imperfection and the imperfection of the knowable world. We can come to understand that we are intended to live in mystery, that we cannot through our own efforts overcome that mystery, but we can learn in faith that the mystery is in the end benign. (Do any of the great philosophies or religions indeed teach the contrary?)

The philosophers of the high Enlightenment sometimes seem to believe that reason could grasp the truth, but they did this by separating out the things that reason or science could know from those that it could not. Most of the great ones, the likes of Thomas Hobbes, Isaac Newton, René Descartes, John Locke, and Immanuel

Kant, knew that their methods could not help us to understand vast realms of yearning. Like Aristotle, their point was to enable us to make the most of our resources, to make us aware of the real—and astonishing—extent of our powers.

Granted, some scientists today think that we are closing in on a final theory. Apply quantum physics to the workings of the cosmos, of matter, motion, and the life process, and you explain, well, everything. Reduce humanity to evolutionary biology and the mind to electrochemical impulses and you are done. No mystery remains. But if you asked a thoughtful scientist whether the achievement of such an all-embracing coherent system would in fact resolve the riddle of our existence, he would say, she *should* say, not a chance.

We do not know precisely what we are looking for. But the common testimony of all our philosophy, our science, and our religion is that we have not found out. The striking fact is that all our teachers concur that some things elude our grasp. Persistently, our heritage of thought suggests that the world we live in might be a flawed copy of a real world that is indeed perfect. And we can recognize that we can think that many of our actions fail to live up to an ideal. We can understand such notions—they are in fact a commonplace of our legacy of ideas—even though we have no real grasp of the greater reality to which they refer.

There is, then, it would seem, far more coherence in the diverse doctrines that have come down to us than we have been led to believe. For the common testimony of all our philosophy, science, and religion is that there is more to reality than is meets the eye. The problem, then, is how we should proceed in the face of our ignorance and the manifest imperfection of the world. At this point the teachings diverge.

Given our awareness of our ignorance, some have recommended that we stick safely to the surfaces. The ancient Sophists, like the modern conservatives, taught that the best we can do is to follow the customs and understandings of our people. The classic materialists and Epicureans, like the modern economists, taught that because all we can be sure of is physical sensation, the sensible thing to do is to feel as good as we can. But the most persistent teaching through all the ages is that we ought to take very seriously our capacity to sense a disparity between the apparent and the real, the customary and the ideal.

The method begins in skepticism. It encourages the individual to doubt the finality of appearances and established understandings. Socrates taught the young to question the finality of the customs of Athens. Descartes taught radical doubt of received philosophy. The language of skepticism always addresses the individual but always also the individual in deliberation with others. The aim of skepticism is not disillusionment. It is instead to invoke our power to sense the difference between the present and the possible, the evident and the real. The trick is to make the familiar seem unfamiliar and the dimly sensed potential quite real.

All our philosophy, our science, and, at the deepest level, our religion rest on an individualist presumption. It is the proponent of a statement about the world, or the good life, who bears the burden of proof, who is obliged to give reasons. The individual, in full exercise of wary skepticism, must decide whether to accept the teaching or not. It is, I say again, a presumption of method that runs from Socrates to contemporary liberalism. It is a way of thinking that entails the incredible assumption that the source of our insight into the reality that underlies appearances is the individual soul. Luther's famous statement of defiance exemplifies this method:

> Unless I am convinced by the testimony of the scriptures or the pure light of reason I am bound by the scripture I have quoted and my conscience is captive to the word of God. I cannot and I will not retract anything since it is neither safe nor right to go against conscience. Here I stand. I can do no other. May God help me.[2]

Every philosophy will in the end recommend a way, a method by which we may find meaning, a guide to making our way through life. And such a recommendation must rest on certain foundations. Every philosophy will speculate about the question of ultimate reality; it will propose a view of underlying order or the character and purposes of God. It makes a guess about what is really going on in the universe. Or it starts by asserting (and it is equally a first premise, a foundation of theory) that it does not know a thing about order, if an order exists at all.

Thus closely related to this view of underlying reality in a philosophy is its epistemology, its theory of the known and knowable. It proposes an idea of method: How we can find out, how we can decide what to do. One philosophy may emphasize the things about which we can be most certain, as in Cartesian rationalism or positivist science. Another may emphasize the qualities of our greatest wonder, as in religious mysticism. Thus we have no complete, comprehensive epistemology that would teach us how to know everything. Each is a rumination on where we might best fix our attention to find out what we humans can about what is actually the nature of our situation. Every theory of knowledge is a conjecture about the relationship of human capabilities and the meaning of the world. So it involves a decision about which human capabilities are most important to nurture and develop if we are to understand.

This is the method of all the great works in our tradition of philosophy. We begin with a conception of ultimate reality. We create an image of ourselves and what we can know. Everyday science and practical reason also use this method. And this method is pertinent to our deliberations about the public philosophy, on the questions we must ask about the legacy that we intend to pass on to coming generations. We become aware of the significance of the method when we sense a gap between appearance and reality, when we begin to feel, uneasily, that the images and understandings promoted by the powerful seem designed to distort our understanding in ways that promote their interests and their power. We become aware of the significance of the method when we begin to suspect that the "common understandings" that popular culture promotes are not understandings at all, that they are taking us far from the truth, far from what we need to know in order to live well.

The public philosophy is inevitably part of our larger speculations and our wonder. You derive a politics, an economics, and an ethic from a metaphysics and an epistemology. You cannot do it the other way around. The hypocrisy is immediately apparent if you start from a political program and jury-rig a view of ultimate reality and of knowledge to fit it. Politics, economics, and ideas of the conduct of everyday life have to follow from the idea of truth or, what amounts to the same thing, our doubts and skepticism that we can find the truth or that any truth exists to find.

The task of political philosophy is to respond to the third primary question, the question of human responsibilities and purposes. The charge of political philosophy is to make sense of our intimations of justice and transform them into a law that we can give to ourselves.

The history of political philosophy is a long effort to justify authority, to give free individuals good reasons to consent to be governed.

You do not write political philosophy if you simply want to persuade people to follow the will of the people in power. Then you write ideology or propaganda. You do not write political philosophy if you think that the rulers descended from the sun or were appointed by the gods. Then you write myth.

Political philosophy cannot speak to the dogmatists, the true believers, or the fanatics who are absolutely convinced that they know what is right. Nor has it anything to say to those who believe that submission is inevitable, a duty laid down in the stars. Political philosophy can only be of interest to people who, assuming themselves to be free, are interested in the question of when they are rightly ruled. The special problem of political philosophy is to produce an answer to that question that is convincing, beyond a reasonable doubt.

This is the peculiarly daunting problem of political philosophy, and it accounts for the special form that it has taken through all the ages. Plato first stated the riddle in *The Republic*. What if a few among us did hit on an answer to the question of how to live truly? They would then be entitled to rule, for they would do so in the name of truth and justice. But the problem is how would those of us in the cave—those of us of uncertain knowledge and will— recognize the true rulers? How can the unwise recognize the wise? Frauds and charlatans are many, and we are easy to deceive. We might consent to just about anything, so our compliance means nothing. On the other hand, for the wise to impose their rule by force does not solve the problem. For us to accept that we are justly ruled, we must understand justice.

The problem that structures the enduring work of political philosophy is how to justify authority. And the way that the problem has been put throughout our history rests on a remarkable assumption about human nature. The assumption is that none of us actually knows the meaning and purpose of life, what it would mean to live truly and fully. It is also supposed that we are able to recognize our finitude and fallibility, because we are dimly aware of a possibility of truth and goodness that always eludes our grasp. We can know that we do not understand. All political philosophy is founded on this utterly enchanting and mystical proposition about the human situation.

Some (the Hegelians) have taught that we might learn the answers in the fullness of time. Others (utopians, Marxists) have taught that we might come to live truly if we can understand and remove the impediments, social and mental, that prevent us from doing so. Some (Nietzscheans, existentialists) have thought that the point is to admit the meaninglessness and dismiss the intimations that we keep having that something is greater. Still others (Scholastics, progressive liberals like John Stuart Mill, pragmatists like John Dewey) have been interested in contriving a politics that would enable us to wrest as much meaning as we could from our experience.

But many other political philosophies, including those that have been dominant for much of history, have taken our state of incompleteness and our awareness thereof to be indeterminate, persisting. This is true of the Christians, who stressed our fallen condition. It also is true of many classic liberals, who thought that human nature was pretty much a constant and that, understanding this, we could contrive political mechanisms, constitutional orders, market-like arrangements that we would recognize as appropriate for people like us, pretty much universally and perpetually.

So political philosophy is best understood as a long consistent inquiry into the question of what kind of politics, what kind of law, we would feel ourselves obliged to accept when we recognize ourselves as we truly are, as creatures who are flawed and groping. The central question—indeed, the only question—of political philosophy is how we should go about governing ourselves and leading worthwhile lives, given that none of us has more than the vaguest conception of what is actually going on.

Those who write political philosophy can advise us. But the question of how we shall frame the public philosophy, and how we shall teach it, is up to us, the elders, in every generation. And what we shall teach inevitably reflects the answers that we intend to give to the primary questions, the questions that humanity must inevitably ask when it awakes.

3

Living Philosophically and Living Well

We are looking for an idea of individuality and freedom that could serve as the basis of our political order and that we would also be proud to teach as a personal philosophy, a way of living.

To put the matter this way instantly creates a serious problem for liberal political theory. Liberalism, after all, is supposed to be impartial among different ways of life. Its very point is to abstain from endorsing, and enforcing, specific conceptions of the human good. Yet, as I have already shown, it seems inevitable that we will make some judgment on the purposes of freedom and therefore on the kinds of lives that we want to encourage and discourage.

Liberal political theorists seem to have remarkably different ideas about when individual freedom is well used. The utilitarians seem to suppose that our lives are well lived as an endless calculation of satisfactions. the moral philosopher John Rawls originally taught that the task of the individual was to create a "rational life plan."[1] The best life was one you could live consistently and coherently. In effect, you could give a reasoned account of all your actions. In recent years liberal political theorists have become preoccupied with the problem of intellectual and cultural pluralism. Now it appears that the good life is a matter of becoming embedded in one of the frameworks for understanding and living that is present in your society and of making its ways your own while respecting the rights of others to live by totally different philosophies and moral codes.[2]

All this, to my mind, raises a more basic question. What does it mean to live philosophically? And why do we think that this is a good thing?

Living philosophically may seem to be a grandiose idea. I do not think that we should treat it that way. I think that living philosophically can be understood as an accomplishment that we can see in all kinds of people from every walk of life.

Living philosophically clearly need not mean following a formal doctrine—being consistently and exclusively existentialist, Kantian, positivist, Thomist. (Does anyone actually live this way? Better, should anyone live this way?)

How indeed would you describe your personal philosophy? Is it a single central resolve to act responsibly, to be kind and caring, to be ambitious and successful? Or is it a set of disconnected maxims that you can use to justify whatever course of action seems intuitively right to you at the time? Where did you get your philosophy? Is it all of a piece? Or is it a patchwork, drawn from many sources? Did you make up your philosophy pretty much by yourself? Are you done yet?

Oddly, we seldom ask such question of ourselves or of others. Social science does not study such matters. It simply assumes that people receive their beliefs and values from society. It does not examine how individuals develop their own ideas of worth, meaning, and purpose. Novelists, biographers, and essayists sometimes talk about such things. But the dominant impression is that philosophers create philosophies; ordinary people do not.

Still, writers and teachers through the ages have urged us, earnestly, insistently, to live philosophically. What can this mean? How can philosophy actually help us?

Some would say that the purpose of philosophy is to invest life with meaning. A good philosophy will make life rich. Everything you do will be alive with significance. You will feel deeply, see clearly, live fully. Not to have a philosophy is to move along on the surfaces, going through the motions, doing the expected thing, not seeing much more point to life's activities, great or small.

Yet you do not need a philosophy to invest life with meaning, satisfaction, and a sense of being worthwhile. A culture can provide all of this perfectly well. You can lead an enormously satisfying life, and most people do, simply by doing all the things that are normal and expected, by respecting custom and tradition, by carrying out your duties and playing out your roles, by thinking and caring about the ordinary and the commonplace. Many people who live happy and productive lives do precisely that. They find it perplexing to be asked to reflect, to question, to probe deeper. They do not yearn, nor are they restless. The unexamined life can indeed be worth living. The only problem is that it will not be your own.

However, in our day and age the unexamined life, the conforming and conventional life, is incredibly complex and demanding. It requires great powers of discernment, great mental agility. We must balance competing obligations. We must respond as expected to highly diverse and subtle cues.

Each day we are expected to shift gears many times. We bring one mind-set, one set of values and beliefs, one philosophy, if you will, to work. We live by another one entirely at home. We profess a third during religious worship. We affirm and try to practice yet another in civic life. We know we must not confuse these outlooks and commitments, these habits and skills. Bring home the habits of the workplace—say, policing or lawyering—and the results would be disastrous. Conversely, relate to your colleagues through your philosophy of parenting, and they will quickly ask you to stop.

What we learn, and early, is a confirmed contextuality. We learn that understanding is fragmentary; things are not supposed to add up. We find this out in school. Knowledge is plural. The approaches to learning are diverse and have little overall coherence. Each subject calls for a separate response. We must approach science, literature, and mathematics with distinct attitudes and skills and, for that matter, beliefs. You do not give a subjective impression of a mathematical proof. You do not claim that your reading of a text is axiomatically correct. We find out that what we learn from our religion has absolutely no bearing on what we learn in school and the other way around. We learn to keep the spheres separate and distinct.

We become adept at playacting. Our aim is to do the "appropriate" thing. We want to avoid appearing inept and awkward. We shift our point of view, our beliefs and concerns, to fit the circumstances. This is not hypocrisy. It seems moral in a sense; it is what society asks of us. We do not expect life to have integrity. We do not expect all these engagements, tasks, affirmations, commitments to add up. We do not actually expect life to have a meaning.

Yet the fact—which I will dwell on at length herein—is that living a life of complete conformity is impossible. You are bound to interpret. You are bound to make personal judgments about the things that you are called upon to do. If you are thus fated to be at least partly autonomous, why not do this thoughtfully, which is to say, philosophically?

INDIVIDUALITY AND LIVING PHILOSOPHICALLY

Living philosophically means trying to do better than sheer conformity and simple adaptation to expectations. Living philosophically means at least becoming aware that all these customs and expectations and methods are at best working approximations of a deeper purpose and understanding that we have to come to terms with in our own way.

The one clear teaching of our liberal public philosophy is that your personal philosophy is something that you are supposed to find—indeed, create—for yourself. There is no one right way to live philosophically. You are not expected to question everybody you meet in the manner of Socrates or to wander around in the woods in the manner of Thoreau. Certainly, it does not mean that you must be conspicuously grave and serious. The yearning to know and to live truly does not take the same form in each person. No single version of the quest exists—though it is essential that you undertake a quest.

Living philosophically means living in awareness and amazement. But we are all aware of and amazed by different things. Some are amazed by clouds and some by computer chips. Some are amazed by their own strength. Some are amazed at the mystery of God, but you do not have to be unless it suits you. And no one is capable of living in constant amazement. We get to pick and choose. We have to take most things for granted.

Living in awareness means penetrating surfaces, being suspicious of accepted meanings and rituals, turning things over, trying to get closer to how things truly are. Living philosophically means not being gullible, for gullibility is a close kin of servility. But surely, being generally wary and suspicious is no virtue. We do not question everything. Trust is also part of the philosophic life. We have to decide what is worth questioning and what we should accept.

Some principles of right and wrong apply to all humanity. But one morality applies to you alone. It is a variant of the universal ethic, designed for your case. You are a distinctive bundle of talent and temperament. Some things are expected of you and some things are forgiven. You have a gift for writing. You are awkward in crowds. What you should do is different from what anyone else should do.

Even the stern rules of good and evil apply to us differently, for we are differently tempted. It may be easy for you to avoid the lusts of ambition and greed. Others, we know, are driven from birth by envy and a craving for fame and success. Those who join religious orders know that for some celibacy is easy, for others it is a constant trial and burden.

Right and wrong are not relative on this understanding, but they do apply differently to different people. Our internal struggles are not all the same. Some paths of rightfulness are easy for us to walk. Others betray us, expose our frailty. If we are wise, we understand this in ourselves and others. But why does philosophy so seldom discuss this individuality of morality?

What shall we, then, teach the young about the work of fashioning a personal philosophy? Is it not astonishing how little our elders taught us about this matter? Liberalism is very clear that we have the right to create a plan for life. It tells us nothing about how to go about doing it.

In all that is to come, I shall try to come to terms with this issue. At this point we need but a few preliminary observations.

I do not think that we want to teach that our personal philosophy is unique, that it fits us and us alone. It is no more than an adaptation, an interpretation, of a whole legacy of thought that pertains to other people as well.

A personal philosophy is not simply an exercise in self-understanding. Rather, it is an effort to understand where we are, in this case the nature of our "situatedness" and who we are, our sense of our own particularity, and, then, what we are indeed expected to do, given what we take to be the nature of things. This is not something that we can figure out all by ourselves. We need all the help we can get. We need to draw on all our traditions, our public philosophy, every element that our elders have handed down to us, all that they have tried to teach us.

Each individual is unique. Living philosophically is something that we have to do in our own way. But living philosophically is a work that we have in common. We all have to do this, and for this reason we are mutually responsible to one another in our quest. Because we see things differently, because we are differently aware and amazed, for the very reason of our diversity we can teach one another and learn from one another.

Our work is a work of inquiry. We must try things out on one another, test our intimations and understandings, see if they make sense to anyone else. We must rely on others to check us and question us, for we are all prone to fantasy and illusion when left too long alone with our thoughts.

No one model of the philosophic life, no one way of living philosophically, exists. But do we not have an obligation to explain ourselves, to make our quest for meaning intelligible? I believe so. We are all trying to find out simultaneously. We have minds that work in similar ways. We live in a similar world. This is, I think, why reason is important to the philosophic life. We have a duty to explain ourselves. It is, perhaps, not morally wrong to be incoherent. It is simply not helpful. All we have to offer is the sense that we are able to make to the others. And we depend on the others, all the others, for generations and generations back to the beginning, for the sense that we will make of ourselves and the world. We live to pass meaning along.

Our work is a work of discovery, of trying to get behind the surfaces, trying to find out a little more about how things actually are and trying to get a clearer sense of what we really should be doing. In other words, the aim is to get a little closer to the truth.

This all begins when we realize that our thoughts are not the final thoughts, our ways of working not necessarily the best ways of working, our music not the final music, our manners just a passing phase in the long search for gentleness and respect among people.

To be able to see the universal behind the particular, the form behind the function, the purpose behind the practice can give us a whole new bearing on what it means to be here, alive, and in the world. It can lead us to the reenchantment of the world. We can awake to mystery.

PHILOSOPHY AND DEMOCRACY

We certainly believe that some individuals can come alive in vision and in wonder, to be creative, ingenious, and deft and thus open to new possibilities for human endeavor. But now we reach the question that has haunted political philosophy through the ages. Is it possible for a people to live thus, in a state of self-consciousness, of inquiry? Is it possible to create a philosophical democracy?

John Dewey certainly thought so, and the optimism of his belief in the potential intelligence of democracy lingered as an extraordinary strand in American political thought until quite recently. Karl Marx and John Stuart Mill, in different ways and with different hesitations and ambiguities, also thought that the way of inquiry might become the way of democracy. But Plato, who is father of us all, had his doubts. In most readings he seemed to believe that the life of philosophy was open only to very few, that most of humanity would live lives mainly of passion and necessity. Democracy, indeed, was a threat to philosophy. This is the significance of the trial of Socrates. Ordinary people are comfortable with the familiar trappings of the cave. They will resist the philosopher who tries to bring them out into the light.

Was it the witless superficial servility of the life of the crowd or harsh material necessity, the conditions of life in the crowd, that made so many think that the best life, the philosophic life, was possible only apart from the way of life of ordinary people, away from the crowd? Friedrich Nietzsche thought the former. Democratic politics led inexorably to the triumph of the "last man," the absolutely ordinary person who lives for momentary pleasure alone. The aims of politics become comfort and security. These become the highest purposes of life.[3]

But Aristotle, and in a different sense Marx, thought it was not incapacity but necessity that made a life guided by reflection so rare. Philosophy required leisure, and the life of most of humanity was one of debilitating toil. Aristotle's conception of the household, in its extreme form, was a political economic unit that required the organization of slaves, workers, and women so that one man, the owner, could be free.[4] And Marx dreamed that when capitalism had overcome scarcity, humanity would at last be free to live "authentically."

There is, I think, a better way of looking at this problem. This is to say that I cannot imagine an individual, or a people, living in a constant state of awareness, living philosophically, all the time. Everyone knows that the moments of insight come, if they come at all, in sidelong glimpses, glancing illuminations, in the midst of doing all sorts of other things. To be sure, awareness is most likely to come to those who are prepared for it, to those who are looking in the right direction. But awareness is not a constant state for anybody. (Mystics, in particular, know and teach this.) And foreseeing to whom it will come is quite difficult. Awareness is not the prerogative of any class or profession. The elites, those who have been specially prepared and nurtured, may fail to grasp the point at the moment of truth, while the rank amateur may seize it.

As Aristotle, William James, and many others have taught, we live most of our lives by habit. Reducing our striving for good performance to repeatable routine is efficient. Only when our established ways of doing things fail to work do we face puzzlement and perplexity, and then we inquire—or we are paralyzed, blocked from action.[5] The whole point of education, I believe, is to teach people how to inquire when things go wrong, rather than breaking down in despair or joining the cult or the mob.

Some think that the philosophic life is a life of contemplation and that it is incompatible with an active, public life. It is a life apart. That may be true for some people. But the philosophic life can also be a life lived in the midst of the world, in traffic. In fact, would not a life filled with experience, achievement, and sorrow and pain, a life thrown in actively with all sorts of people, doing all sorts of things, be more apt to generate philosophy, deep insight, than a life of solemn contemplation? I know that many of our greatest religious teachers have urged withdrawal from the world. I simply take a different view.

In any event, such a view makes a belief in the compatibility of philosophy and democracy tenable. Do not imagine true democracy as a state of transformed human consciousness, of enlightened, rapturous, responsible citizens sitting about all day in the forum, deliberating the public good. Rather, picture democracy as the work of ordinary people who, when they face predicaments, will reflect on what they are doing, will puzzle and try to improve and perfect their ways of doing things, rather than plod on mindlessly or lose their senses.

If nothing else, living philosophically means living thoughtfully rather than carelessly. It means considering the opinions of others, weighing them, asking whether what someone else believes may actually be better than your current thoughts. It means thinking through potential consequences carefully, warily. It means seeing clearly the innumerable efforts to manipulate and deceive that are abroad in the land and treating them with the contempt that they deserve. Living philosophically means trying to find the truth of the matter.

How many are capable of living as reflective individuals? Who knows? It may be a majority or it may be a minority. But the idea that only a few can live authentically, while the masses are condemned to live mindlessly by bread and circuses, is a shallow conceit. To be sure, there will always be those who for various reasons cannot cope independently, and some, I fear, who wish not to live for themselves but seek the shelter of a life of subordination. This is what Aristotle actually meant, I think, by "natural slavery."

In any event, the qualities of true individuality are not rare, and we cannot decide them in advance. They are not an attribute of class or education or refinement. Perfectly ordinary people can see the full significance of a kitten or of light on a clear creek, of an unjust law, or of people who do not deserve what fate has dealt them. Perfectly ordinary people can think critically and creatively about the ways of their craft or their community. At the crucial moment the seemingly most gifted may act thoughtlessly, impulsively, while the seemingly least reflective may patiently dissect the problem and come up with the solution. For the democrat, these things are not a matter of faith but experience.

So the purpose of affirming these special human qualities as part of the public philosophy is not a utopian appeal for complete social transformation. This is not a call for us to achieve a new state of consciousness, to transcend, collectively, the limitations of our age. Rather, it turns out that the philosophic life, astonishingly, may rest on quite ordinary human possibilities. The problem, then, is that the images of humanity contained in our most prominent political theories—the self-interest of utilitarian economics, the conservative view that we can be nothing more than what social role and culture prescribe—do not represent human normality but what we normally take to be human aberration. We do not want to teach the children that these are the best ways of life. The best life, incredibly, turns out to be the way of life that many try to live most of the time, and on some days or for some hours many actually succeed in living it.

PART II

Individuality

4

What Is Freedom For?

We are under no obligation to teach a particular system of beliefs about public purpose and the meaning of life. Our liberal political theory is itself heterodox and contradictory. To pretend that any one version of it is authentic would be disingenuous. Any version of this common tradition that we presume to teach will, then, inevitably be an interpretation. It is well for us to recognize this and be candid about it. We are, of necessity, free to frame our own legacy.

Thus we must go back to the beginning and reconsider all the basic questions. So let us now ask, as artlessly as possible: Why do we value individual freedom so highly? What do we take to be the purpose of freedom? What is it for? These are, I believe, the essential questions. I think that they will take us to the heart of the matter. Everything else depends on our answers to them.

Is it our intent to teach that our highest common purpose, the aim that gives meaning to all our efforts, is that people should be left alone to do just as they please? It might seem so. Liberalism often conveys a strong belief in personal independence, a determination to go it alone and to be left alone. The idea of rugged individualism is still vivid in our culture. But is this the essence of our idea of freedom? Is this the idea of freedom that we wish to pass along?

Perhaps this starkly individualist picture of how life is to be lived is not at all what we intend. Perhaps it is not a logical implication of liberal political theory at all. It may be an accidental, indeed regrettable, by-product of the way that liberal political theory deals with the problem of truth.

Classically, liberalism achieved its "self-evidence" as an entailment of our skepticism, our doubt. If our final view of the human situation is that no mortal philosopher kings exist, that neither a specified elite nor the community by consensus can reveal the meaning of our existence and our final purposes on Earth, if these things are in fact forever shrouded in mystery—which is, indeed, what both our secular and our religious traditions insist—then individuals must, of necessity, define their meanings and their purposes for themselves. Any public philosophy founded on a claim to know these final things is a deceit. The only just regime is one that permits individuals to pursue their own conception of the good.

The truth of classical liberalism is often thought to be grounded on this one axiomatic certainty. Those who take classical liberalism to be a rational imperative, a universal proposition to which all humanity will in the end consent, tend to appeal to this first principle. The method is the purest Cartesianism. Once you have doubted until you can doubt no more, a single truth emerges. All the rest is a matter of working out the implications.

But it turns out that this is not quite enough. You cannot actually derive a political theory from the premise of neutrality alone. To fashion a plausible view of the legitimate regime, you have to make some assumptions about the characteristics of humanity that should lead people to accept one kind of political order rather than another. Thus you need a theory of human nature, some conception of the traits, qualities, and capacities that best characterize our behavior, or those that we should encourage or discourage if we are to make the most of our humanity. You have to make some assumptions about where our reason would naturally lead us. Thus no political theory is actually impartial about the human condition.

In their assumptions about human nature, most political theories are sternly reductionistic. The object is to find some thin, spare universal proposition that we might plausibly accept, amid all our diversity, as a rock bottom characterization of our kind. But such assumptions turn out to be highly contentious. We can easily contradict them, and we are soon thrown back into those unsolvable dichotomies that have plagued our thought through the centuries and that we wasted many evenings debating in our youth, when we first learned to try making categorical statements about our nature. Are we really free individuals, or are our selves the product of social conditioning? Are we basically nature or nurture? Selfish or altruistic? Competitive or cooperative? And so on, indefinitely.

In what is to come, I examine four conceptions of individuality and freedom. I could have included others, but I believe that these are the most familiar rival images of humanity that underlie our present debates about the public philosophy.

The issue is this: Whatever the utility of these ideas of human nature in framing a political theory, would we accept any of them as the foundation for a philosophy of everyday life? Would we want to teach future generations to understand their lives along the lines that any of these theories prescribe? Would we want them to learn to think according to the ideas of reason taught therein? I think that we will be reluctant to give unconditional assent to any of these theories. In some cases I think we will find their implications appalling.

No political philosophy is neutral about different ways of life. So the question of which human capabilities we wish to cultivate and which we wish to discourage is inescapable. We are under no obligation to accept any prevailing doctrines of human nature or natural reason. None can claim to be rationally necessary.

RAW UTILITARIANISM

Now, to say that individuals should pursue an idea of the good sounds somewhat nobler, more elevated, than to say that they should do as they please. However, in much of liberal political thought these distinctions cannot hold. Who has the authority to say which aims are higher? Some may live for immediate sensual gratification. Others may seek the sublime. It is all the same in the end. Thus we might as well say that people pursue what they value and try to avoid what they find repugnant. Which is to say that all human aims can be reduced to self-interest: We seek pleasure and try to avoid pain.

This raw Benthamite utilitarianism is widespread today. This is about all we teach anymore about economics, and it is much of what we teach about philosophy and politics. We tell the young that the best way to explain human actions, individual and social, is to analyze interests. We teach them that achieving the good life is a calculation of personal satisfactions. We tell them to approach ethical and political dilemmas through a calculation of costs and benefits to the affected parties.

There is, some will protest, an ethical utilitarianism. The good person lives to create the greatest good for the greatest number or perhaps, as the British philosopher Karl Popper wisely suggested, to reduce suffering as much as possible. In some guises such an ethic sounds good. But putting it into practice is hard. I note that when most people start thinking about the "greatest good," they shift to Aristotelianism and start asking about what is really good for people, which is against the rules of this particular game. Utilitarian philosophy has always been quite vague on how to compare individual preferences and aggregate them. And for most economists the greatest good is simply growth.

Ethical utilitarianism is puzzling. When the personal good is part of the general good, what becomes of the personal good if you are living for the general good? Should you first calculate your personal good and then ask whether it is compatible with the general good? This might result in a rough-and-ready Kantianism, where you would ask, "What if everyone did it?" before each action. But this is not what most utilitarians intimate.

Pure political Benthamism seems to suppose a different way of thinking for rulers and citizens. Ordinary people simply pursue their self-interest, and the legislators try to contrive institutions that will maximize general happiness. But this seems an odd division of humanity, and it does not tell us what will happen if the two modes of reason contaminate one another. What happens if the people start placing the general interest above their personal desires (which, curiously, makes utilitarianism impossible, for without personal interests there can be no general interest)? Or what if the rulers confuse their personal satisfaction with the general happiness, which seems not unlikely, given human frailty?

Pure utilitarianism, as a philosophy, is not precisely the same thing as classic free-market political economy. Indeed, the two schools have clashed on many points. Ethical utilitarianism often finds free-market outcomes unacceptable. Free-market advocates think that utilitarian critiques of market society are intrusive and officious. Nonetheless, in our times a look at the merits of this case is worthwhile because enough people believe that the greatest good for the greatest number would arise automatically if all pursued their calculated self-interest in an ideal market system.

Bear in mind that, for pure classical liberals, not just the economy but all human relationships should be based on market-like arrangements. To be rightful, all human institutions must reflect the conditions of contract: voluntary, deliberate, informed choice in the presence of genuine alternatives. This should be the basis for religion, the family, education, culture, and science, as well as commerce. (The state, which is an involuntary organization, must show that it rests on a virtual contract, one that all reasonable people would find it in their interest to join. That is another story, which we will turn to shortly.)

If individuals are always free to leave an undesired relationship for an equally valued alternative, the problem of power evaporates. If individuals are truly free to go elsewhere, tyranny, exploitation, or subjugation in employment, church, or family cannot exist. The most humble individuals are as mighty as the great corporations so long as they are free to walk out of the GM salesroom and go to Ford. Bosses cannot exploit employees so long as they can find an equivalent job. Or so the story goes.

Thus the good society arises spontaneously. It is the sum of all the preferences of all the individuals among the abundant options which are the fruit of the entrepreneurial energies that market incentives and rewards release. The market society produces opportunities and goods (again, of commodities, of services, of faith, of wisdom, of beauty) in just the proportion that people actually want them. No elite decides what people should have.

Each individual choice counts the same. The market is neutral among different ways of life. It meets the skeptical requirement, the acknowledgment of our ignorance of our own meaning that is the foundation of our philosophy.

The market society is not extravagant. It is frugal. Consumers cannot demand the impossible, abundance beyond the capacity of society. No one can require the producers to produce more than is profitable. The market provides the best mechanism for squaring the satisfaction of human interests with environmental sustainability. It will naturally substitute more abundant resources for scarcer ones. The effete, the snobs, the self-appointed elites cannot demand that anyone cater to their special tastes unless they make it worth someone's while to do so. The market is egalitarian.

Market society gives meaning and purpose to life. It offers many opportunities, many niches, where you can make the most of your talents. Market society is competitive, and the object is success. But inherent in the market ideal is a strangely familiar morality and a sense of justice. Those who serve others best, *in the personal estimation of those others,* will be rewarded, honored, esteemed. Those who produce what others want will see their stores crowded, their books purchased, their churches and stadiums full. Those who produce what people do not much want—hand-dipped candles, recondite scholarly tomes—will receive paltry rewards. The society does not have to answer the historically intractable question, What is justice? The market, by its own operation, creates it.

As I say, the model of the market society, in which all choices are equal and the common good is the natural product, is an ideal, a myth, a utopia. If you think that the ideal actually represents the workings of any capitalist society, you will believe anything. We understand perfectly well that what a capitalist society actually produces is not necessarily what people want, in their own deliberate calculations of self-interest, but what mammoth corporations have found it most profitable to produce. Therefore the market offers far more fast food, sleazy entertainment, and obscure electronic gear and far less affordable housing, good food, and decent education than there would be if we had, let us say, a relatively equal distribution of income and an ethic that gave incentives to quality rather than profit.

We also understand that part of what we pay for the products that we buy (as a kind of tax, for it is not actually part of the cost of production) goes to fund a remarkably elaborate effort to manipulate our tastes so that we will prefer what enterprise finds it most profitable to produce.

Part of the ethic of the market, as we have seen, is to believe that those who rise to the top do so on the basis of merit. Competition fairly decides who is worthier, who is deserving of income, honor, recognition, and social status. Aside from the obvious fact that success in modern society has much to do with class, contacts, social background, and simple luck, we have other reasons to think that this is not a particularly attractive social ideal.

A meritocratic society defines success as striving and winning. It has little to do with striving for excellence as an end in itself, with craftsmanship, care, and conscientiousness, with doing the right thing. Furthermore, when a society construes all of life as a race, only a few can be winners. Most people must think themselves failures. This is not a philosophy that encourages self-respect. This is in fact a wretched personal ethic.[1]

Liberalism denounced traditional society because the elders presumed to prescribe the values, the way of life, for all the people. Now I wonder if we are not back in the same fix all over again. It may be that the powerful have presumed to teach us an ethic of striving competition, consumer hedonism, and uncaring self-seeking against our better judgment.

What is interesting is how easily we all recognize what Marx called "the contradictions of capitalism." And it is fascinating that the very same philosophy of individual choice, contract, and market systems that provides the justification for advanced capitalism is the source of our most devastating criticisms of it.

All this is familiar. The question at this point is simply whether this is the everyday ethic that we wish to pass on to future generations. After all, we do have other options to consider.

CIVILITY

Another variant of classical liberal thought, another way of looking at the significance of liberal freedom, is available: the view that reasonable people will recognize that to realize the fruits of freedom requires the goodwill and cooperation and the love and friendship of others. Even the most mechanical advocate of raw utilitarianism should recognize that we all must restrain our personal pursuit of self-interest in recognition of the reciprocal right of others. The free society, then, would be one of mutual respect, tolerance, and civility, a peaceable kingdom. We could pretty much reduce the legitimate role of government to protecting and interpreting the rights of individuals. Government would have a background role, that of a nightwatchman and a judge.

The image is familiar. This is, I believe, the basis of much of our everyday, working morality. This is roughly what our courts mean when they ask whether an individual can tell the difference between right and wrong. And that means, by the way, that the person who actually practices raw utilitarianism, who thinks that life is all about maximizing self-interest, would not be thought a rational calculator but morally deficient, unfit to stand trial. The Benthamite and Lockean versions of liberalism intertwine in all kinds of odd ways in Western thought. One is the basis of our economics, and the other is the basis of our law. We mix these ideas together in strange combinations. Often, we do not even notice the contradictions.

This version of liberal freedom is familiar too, so familiar in fact that we usually are oblivious of the extraordinary portrait of human nature that frames it. Nor do we reflect much on the unusual exercises that philosophers have produced to try to prove to all humankind that this is indeed the path of natural reason. For this version of liberal reason is grounded in another effort to derive one certainty from a starting point of absolute skepticism about the ability of anyone to understand the meaning of life and thus to have the right to prescribe a way of life to another.

The philosophical exercise begins with a peculiar thought experiment. You are asked to imagine yourself—and everybody else—in a state of nature. You are not part of a society. You are under no law. You have not been socialized. You are a truly free and autonomous individual. In such circumstances what morality would you accept as natural and binding? Under what circumstances would you voluntarily accept the authority of another to decide what you might do and what you should do?

The object is to find a solution that all would agree is reasonable. And the crucial question in following such exercises is whether you, personally, would accept the solution, without reservation or qualification. Those who write such philosophies stand or fall on the personal transformation. If you are not persuaded, all this is but another interesting idea. Needless to say, no version of social contract theory has ever won universal assent. But, then, it is unlikely that all the critics have entered fully into the spirit of the experiment.

The first effort was Thomas Hobbes's *Leviathan* of 1651, which remarkably anticipates the obvious response to raw utilitarianism. Assume that we are all in fact self-interested utility maximizers, that our nature is to engage in a restless quest, as Thomas Hobbes had it, for "power after power that endeth only in death." But were that the case, would we not naturally recognize that each of us constitutes a threat to every other, that each of us would evaluate every other as a potential means to our ends, and each of us would warily try to resist subjugation or enslavement? All human relations would be tense, mistrustful, deceptive, always on the verge of becoming "a war of all against all." Would we not realize that life in such a world of unrestrained self-interest would be "solitary, poor, nasty, brutish, and short"? Would we not, then, as a matter of simple calculation of personal utility, see the advantage of restraint, tolerance, and cooperation? And would we not also recognize that our ideas of right and wrong were so bound up with our personal advantage that we must give up the right of moral judgment to an impersonal sovereign, who would determine our rights and purposes and enforce them?[2]

Most who read Hobbes are appalled by the conclusion that he drew, that we should find it reasonable to submit to absolute authority. (Though all sorts of contemporary relativists, including many pure democrats, have to end up in something like Hobbes's position.) Thus John Locke, who followed Hobbes's method in the *Second Treatise of Civil Government* (1690) but argued that reasonable individuals should only accept a government that protected their rights better than they could by themselves, became the historic founder of this dominant habit of our thought and the father of liberalism.

Locke's argument picks up where Hobbes's left off. If we are reasonable about our self-interest in the way that Hobbes assumes, if we see the personal advantage in restraint and goodwill instead of persistent fear and conflict, then life in the state of nature would be generally peaceful, cooperative, and civil. Actually, our only need for government would be to protect us in those instances where we personally were not reasonable or against those who will not or cannot be reasonable. Most of the time we can govern ourselves through voluntary cooperation. We have no need for an absolute sovereign.

The reasonableness of goodwill and prudence is usually taken to be the essence of Locke. But I think there is something deeper in Locke. I think he is trying to demonstrate a very special vision of the moral nature of humanity.

Remember that we are still in the state of nature. We have no culture, and we have no political tradition. All of which is to say that what we find right and wrong to be in the state of nature is naturally right and wrong. It will arise from the moral law within us. And thus it will be universal. The moral law may vary in its content with time and circumstances, but it will not vary in its essential character. And thus the free individual is competent, when in a state of detachment from the particularities of culture, to judge the worthiness of culturally defined morality.

Thus Locke seems to be saying that morality is more than cultural contrivance. Even apart from and before culture we are capable of recognizing that murder is wrong, that we have a right to live, that it is natural for people to determine their own purposes, that we have a right to liberty, and that subjugation and enslavement are naturally wrong. (I recognize Locke's ambiguities about slavery, but that is another story.)

We are, then, natural moral agents. An intuition of justice is programmed into us. We recognize that it would be unfair to claim a right that we did not extend to others.

The stumbling block is always property. Locke suggests that it is natural for us to recognize that a person is entitled to appropriate and use "that with which they have mixed their labor." Now consider. Assume that someone, through great toil and effort, has erected a sturdy cabin in our state of nature. Assume also that a great hulking loafer, armed with an ax, has been hanging around throughout the construction. As the last pieces are fit into place, the oaf rises, ambles over to the builder, and says, "Get out of here. That's mine now." I think Locke's point is that we would be shocked, automatically and naturally outraged, even had we no customs or law of property. (I know all the amateur anthropological counters to this argument, all the tales of tribes with communal wives, communal whales, and communal cottages. But if you examine those traditions closely, I think you will find that they have very clear ideas about fair shares and cheating.)

Locke actually attaches three conditions to the right of property. All three must be met in order to find an appropriation from nature fair and rightful. The first is labor. The second is that we actually use what we have appropriated, not waste it. The third is that we leave "as much and as good" for others. The usual commentary on the second condition is that by introducing money and trade, so that we do not actually have to consume what we produce, Locke legitimizes economic inequality. The third principle is said to be archaic—when Locke was writing, England had much vacant land. But there is another way of looking at this. Locke, I believe, can be read as saying that we will find waste and profligacy morally wrong. And I think the third condition implies that the right of property must be universal: All must have access to the resources of nature. Again, we will recognize a monopoly of wealth as inherently unjust.

Lockean liberalism is generally associated with an unintrusive minimal state, which mainly enforces individual rights and thus underwrites the gross inequalities of the capitalism that we know so well. But another reading of Locke leads to the view that inequalities that suppress liberty, or deny to some the right to seek well-being through work and effort, are morally wrong and require redress, perhaps radical reform. Locke, I believe, can correctly be quoted on both sides of the great argument between the liberalism of the minimal state and the liberalism of the activist, positive state, the state that would secure the equal rights of all. Locke indeed is the source of the very structure of this fundamental political argument. His descendants are properly both Adam Smith and Karl Marx, Milton Friedman and John Rawls.

Is this the everyday philosophy of freedom that we seek? Classic liberalism's proposition that truly free, self-aware individuals will recognize their interdependency with others and thus gladly accept an ethic of mutual restraint and respect is appealing. The liberalism that is founded in Locke seems little less than an elegant philosophic effort to demonstrate as rationally compelling the simplest commandments of our religion and what every parent instinctively tries to teach: Do not cheat, do not betray, do not kill, do not bully, do not steal, respect differences, and (if my reading is correct) do not take more than your fair share.

Yet this ordinary ethic rests on an enlarged view of the moral power within the individual that is quite extraordinary, given the widely accepted presuppositions of contemporary relativism and skepticism. To accept this view is to accept the notion that a rather coherent ethical ideal is born within the individual and is not the product of convention or culture. It is to say that we are in fact moral agents and that to see the human situation as it truly is is to understand ourselves as all members of a kingdom of ends. To accept Locke, I believe, you have to accept also a lot of Immanuel Kant.

So the great question is whether this everyday ethic is true. If it is, universal human rights apply everywhere. Genocide is wrong, as are all forms of subjugation and exploitation, as is the appropriation of the product of labor either by the state or the dominant class. In this case the practices of some cultures are morally wrong. We cannot practice universal cultural tolerance. Some things are objectively intolerable.

Or is this philosophy of rights simply a historic artifact of certain Western peoples? In that case other cultures have a right to define the human situation any way they please. (Though, of course, such a doctrine of natural fairness as mutual respect among cultures seems eerily like the idea of natural fairness among individuals that I have just discussed.)

There is a further question about this liberal philosophy. Is this a sufficient ethic, an adequate guide to everyday life? Some argue that this teaching of self-restraint and mutual respect, civility, may be appropriate as a minimal political morality, but it seems to suggest a way of life, a human style, that is impersonal, detached, and distanced. It does not teach us much about passion or engagement or intimacy or tragedy or play or laughter or creativity. As the political theorist Nancy Rosenblum says, we may need "another" liberalism, for this one "does not take individuality, spontaneity, and expressivity into account. Its political society is cold, contractual, and unlovely, without emotional or aesthetic appeal."[3] And the legal scholar and political economist Philip Selznick believes that the responsible "civility" that liberalism teaches needs the counterweight of "piety," "a deep reverence and respect for human interdependence and the continuity between humanity and nature."[4]

How might we teach this balance between civility and piety? Here we see the need for precise expression, for our words can betray us and lead us to seem to endorse conceptions of life that are far from what we intend. If liberal restraint implies cold impersonality, something is wrong with our expression of the ideal. Yet *piety* may suggest zealotry, or unthinking surrender to a cause or creed.

Again, liberalism cannot be neutral. It must teach that being detached and thoughtful is better than giving up your identity to a charismatic leader or extinguishing individuality in a tradition or culture.

We have much to ponder here. Obviously, even the most familiar doctrines are not fully satisfactory in defining the philosophy that we seek. And we must consider other positions before we try to resolve the matter.

POSTMODERN DISENCHANTMENT

We could carry the line of reasoning that begins in doubt much further. The one great certainty that liberalism derives from skepticism is that all individuals must have the right to determine how they will live. Today the great truth that the postmodern critical theorist sees is that none of our systems of philosophy or science or religion, none of our practices, conventions, or techniques, has any legitimate power over us. Realizing this, we are free in the most radical sense to defy all convention, to define our own destiny, to live as we please. At first glance this thought would seem to have a good deal in common with liberalism. In fact it does not.

This line of argument begins in modern times with Friedrich Nietzsche. Some existentialist philosophers shared the view. As usual, there are ancient precedents. Protagoras, and the Sophists generally, had a similar theory of knowledge. For this generation Michel Foucault is the acknowledged high priest. Professors often teach his version of this conception of the problem of freedom to the young today.

For Foucault the distinctiveness of modern society lies in its tight, rationalized social order. To make this system work individuals have to be rigidly disciplined, inhibited, self-controlled. Directing air traffic, performing surgery, or, for that matter, brokering stock allows little room for personal expression or uninhibited impulse. To function well in this society individuals must repress their personal feelings and creative urges. They must fit themselves to the requirements of the system. Those who become "deviant," those who cannot or will not conform, are cajoled or coerced into compliance. Those who will not submit to the requirements of the system are legitimately held apart, in jails or asylums or other facilities for those who cannot quite cope.

Foucault thinks that this is a distinctive quality of modern civilization. Earlier societies could provide more latitude for individual variety. The institutions of earlier ages offered more slack, more room for ambiguity. Foucault's works on the genealogy of morals are indeed brilliant. In them he tells a story of how our "constructions" of madness, criminality, and sexuality have changed over time. In the Middle Ages people thought of madness as folly, an idea charged with intimations of humanity's fallen state and the possibility that the mad might possess a special insight inaccessible to the rest. Today we see madness more as an incapacity to be reasonable, a failure to function appropriately according to the requirements of the intricate web of systematized relations that make up the modern order. The remedy is therapy or separation, the kindly aim is to "normalize" these individuals, to cure them of those distinctive traits that prevent them from fitting in.

With criminality the individual has either willfully transgressed norms of authority or lost control. In the former case the person is justly punished, in the latter justly treated for the disease that causes the failure of self-discipline.[5] To wake up to the actual conditions of modern society is to find yourself in jail. Modern society is profoundly contradictory and deceitful. It announces its aim to be the realization of individual freedom, yet at every turn its institutional design is such as to frustrate that freedom. What is the proper response for someone who recognizes the quandary? Foucault's language is provocative and political. We should seek strategies of "resistance." We should defy "normalization." We should "interrogate" authority.

But what is the positive theory of freedom and individuality here? What is freedom for, in this reading of the world? Officially, the protagonists of this view cannot recommend a way of life. But, like everyone else, in fact they do. The object of freedom is to express yourself, to follow your inclinations, your impulses, your will, your originality, to do all those things that you would do if you were not repressed and disciplined.

The mood is normally vivid and gleeful, a merry kicking over of traces. This is, in essence, romanticism. Nietzsche, who started it all, wrote of the "gay science." Today's advocates join in a wild Whitmanesque celebration of sheer individual variety. We can now embrace humanity in all its discordant extremes. We can now listen to the others whose voices society has suppressed and marginalized.[6]

Is this life of uninhibited self-expression what we seek? Is the object to teach the young to think and to act as differently from one another as possible? Expansive, liberating, and inclusive as this all may seem, it really is a remarkably narrow view of life. It pertains, if it pertains at all, only to those realms where we tell each other how we feel about things, where we express ourselves without inhibition. This may have some bearing on literature and art, but it has nothing to do with the world of work or family or any other realm in which we need to coordinate efforts to achieve a purpose. In most of life *discipline* and *responsibility* cannot be dirty words. Some think this view pertains to politics, but that is true only if we think that the essence of politics is exchanging feelings.

Nothing is obviously "natural" about the uninhibited individuality that postmodern political theory recommends. Modern rational order does require self-control. Perhaps in the end this boils down to a matter of taste and style. So either we take the side of the straight, the square, the good boys and girls who get their assignments in on time, or we take that of the surly, the cool, the defiant, the rowdy, those who snicker in the corners and smoke on the playground.

Again, no political theory is neutral. Yet everything we teach, all our institutions, all our policies, will insinuate some conception of desirable human qualities. But no political theory can demonstrate irrefutably that one way of life is best. The liberal cannot demonstrate that autonomy is better than servility. The Aristotelian cannot prove that a life of fulfillment and flourishing is better than one of frustration. (Is a dissatisfied Socrates better than a satisfied fool?) So the best we can do is decide matters self-consciously, fully aware that we are making choices on behalf of other people.

If we are to encourage individuality in any form, we are going to have to teach the young a certain wariness of the power and interest that lurks within institutions and ideas. We do not want them to be gullible. But do we want them to suspect all discipline and all system? All human skill, all craft, all relationship requires system and rules. Do we, in fact, think of learning a skill, an art, or a method as something that reduces our individuality or as something that expands our capabilities, that enhances our relationships and our usefulness to others?

We are getting close to the heart of the matter. Some people, we know, are habitually too credulous. Others are debilitated by temperamental suspicion. It is a fine art to discern consistently and accurately when system and order enhance and when they diminish our humanity. This means that we must teach the young the skills of political judgment, and as those of us who have spent our lives at it know, this is a difficult art indeed.

CONSERVATISM

Conservatives and liberals seem to be natural antagonists. For centuries conservatives have seen liberal skepticism and individualism as the source of political breakdown and moral decay. For Edmund Burke the French Revolution demonstrated that liberal ideas beget anarchy and terror. (Burke thought differently of the American Revolution, which he took to be an argument about the rights of Englishmen.) For their part liberals historically have seen conservatives as teaching an oppressive and fearful doctrine of conformity to suffocating conventions of culture, to unexplained and unjustified authority, the authority that just happened to be there.

This a real argument, and it continues to our day. It seems an inherent fracture in our thought, a flaw, a fissure running through all that we know and believe, something that we just cannot seem to reconcile, to resolve.

The liberal presumes that individuals can be autonomous, that they can, on their own, alone, introspective, create a conception of their own being, a plan and a philosophy of life. The conservative doubts that this is the case. We are creatures of culture. We take our ideas of the "self" from those around us, from the images and the ideals passed down to us, as I have said, by the elders, by the thoughts, customs, and practices that form our legacy.

What the liberal fears is that the moral that people will draw from this will be one of unconditional obedience and stifling conformity. The individual will be no more than an artifact of culture. The community is the giver of life and its meanings. We must not disdain its gifts.

May I take it that we are not willing to teach that freedom is a chimera? May I presume that we do not believe in absolute cultural determinism, that we are fated to become, obliviously, whatever society would have us become, that we can never think that matters could be otherwise, that we could never decide to make matters otherwise?

The portrait of the conservative as rigid and dogmatic conventionalist, as moral determinist, prone to punish deviance as willful wrongdoing, fearful of inquiry and critical reason, is no caricature. Such people exist. They are the exact counterpart of those who actually believe that raw utilitarianism is true or that pure libertarianism is morally correct. We can say little to those who are locked into these categories of thought and can never for a moment imagine that any but the truly deluded could think otherwise.

We have another conservative frame of mind to consider. These are the people who find the teachings of pure skeptical liberalism, the vision of humanity and human reason as no more than calculated hedonism, to be appalling, as they do the postmodern teaching that all systems of thought and meaning are oppressive. These are people who think such starkly extreme individual atomism, such reductionism, which pictures the individual alone, without ties of affection or commitment, is neither an accurate portrait of humanity nor one we want to pass on to the next generation. These conservatives are not them. They are us.

Again, we teach poorly if we insist only on the differences, the incompatibilities in our systems of understanding. There are, to be sure, real dichotomies in our understanding, ways of construing our place in the order of things that we can only have one way or another. But as we have seen, all human thought has large commonalities. The human phenomenon, after all, has determinable characteristics. We are not free to think of it any way we please. We can observe and insist that some images of humanity (including those we are now examining?) simply do not conform to our experience.

Still, the conservative and the liberal, even when not dogmatists, even when seen, perhaps, as different sides of our own minds, do bring different perspectives to the problem of freedom. The conservative still cannot accept the liberal contention that freedom is a product of autonomy, sheer independence. Freedom seems more something that is found in relationship to culture, tradition, social norms and practices. In trying on, accepting, modifying, and refining the possibilities taught by the elders and contained in our culture, we become a "self," a distinctive individual, truly our own being. We cannot do this in isolation. Indeed, the self that we are apt to form in detachment, in estrangement and alienation, is very apt to be warped and bitter, wasted.

So the conservative has a lesson to teach about the purposes of freedom. We become free by finding our own way into a valued place among our people. And this seems well and good, except that it begs the question of who is this *I* who is doing this?

Perhaps the conservative still wants no self left over. Will this conservative then intimate that even when we think we are being creative or defiant, we are in fact following the norms that we have been taught? The American impressionist creates differently than the African sculptor. Of course. And with that we meet reductionism coming at us from the opposite direction, for now everything must be role and culture, not calculated interest.

But is there not something simply human in our capacities as individuals to interpret and decide about culture, to affirm and renounce selectively the teachings of the elders, the legacy of our kind?

Something is left over. It is now apparent that many of the views of the problem of freedom, taught on good authority, prominent in our politics, brought down to us by distinguished philosophies from our past, have circumvented, or tried to explain away, the idea of the moral capacity of the individual, the power of each person to discern truthfulness and distinguish right from wrong. (Locke may be a partial exception, but as we shall see, his understanding of this capacity is far thinner than many have supposed.) The idea of this power runs deep in our heritage. What indeed are we to say about this power? How are we going to include it in our philosophy of individual freedom?

5

Individuals and the Powers Within

There is another way to proceed. Our quest to understand the significance of individual freedom does not have to end with raw hedonism, a minimalist doctrine of rights, conservative conformity, or Nietzschean nihilism. A very different idea of the purpose of individuality and freedom runs through our heritage. This is the view that the individual has a moral power—a capacity to distinguish right from wrong, excellence from error, justice from injustice. Thus the task of individuals is to get in touch with this power, to use it to critically examine the conventions and practices of the culture and to make improvements if they can, to move life, personally and collectively, a bit closer to the best intimations of the soul.[1] That the individual has the power to transcend, and thus to assess, culture is a view that is fundamental to the liberalism of Kant and Hegel, Mill and Dewey, as well as to the individualism of Plato and Aristotle, the Roman Stoics, and all of Christianity. This idea of individuality runs deep through our philosophical heritage. It is, I believe, fundamental to our liberal public philosophy. Yet the moment we ask what, precisely, we intend to teach the young about these powers within the individual, I think we will find that we are beset by doubt and perplexity. Despite the social relativist and determinist intellectual fashions of the moment, most liberals are still willing to speak easily of moral agency and free will, even, perhaps, of the human spirit and the soul. Invoking these powers at the abstract, general level is easy. But when we get down to cases, what do we intend to tell the young about how to find and how to use these powers and how to distinguish the genuine article from its counterfeits?

AUTONOMY

If the moral life requires autonomy and authenticity, what do we actually mean when we invoke these states of being?[2] Some philosophers, Henry Thoreau and Jean-Jacques Rousseau for example, identify autonomy with radical solitariness and disdain for society. More commonly, in political and moral philosophy *autonomy* implies detachment and disinterestedness. The moral ideal is to stand back and stand apart, distancing yourself from interests, attachments, your personal characteristics and temperament, passing judgment from a purely universal and abstract point of view.[3] But when we have stripped ourselves of all "encumbrances" of belief and value, how shall we then decide? Do we assume that we will find the pure image of justice and the human good emergent in the stillness of our souls, surely, purely, inerrantly?

What should we tell the young to listen for when they go inside? The voice within may be the voice of parents, of the tradition, of the schools. Schizophrenics also hear voices, as do all manner of fanatics. And many say that the quest for inwardness will end in perfect silence.

My own view, for whatever that may be worth, is that we need not think of autonomy and detachment only as a kind of settled state of being, a more or less permanent Stoic separation from the confusions and contortions of the world. I think we can understand detachment also as a momentary pause, a drawing back to regain perspective in the midst of action, or what we do when we stand back from a work in progress to take stock. Here the self does not emerge in solitude. Rather, it comes forth, as the psychologist and philosopher George Herbert Mead would have said, in interaction with specific social situations and events.[4]

When I draw back to achieve this kind of detachment, I am not expecting a voice to speak. I am waiting for a pattern to emerge, an image or understanding that will suggest how I am to go on.

This may seem an attitude more intellectual than moral or spiritual, but I honestly believe that I cannot tell the difference. To wait expectantly for something to emerge is obviously the method of creative thought and practical reason. It is also, I believe, the method of meditation, mysticism, and contemplative prayer.[5]

I know also that, when I am struggling with a page or a paragraph (as I am now), the only explanation for my dissatisfaction can be the disparity between what is written on the page and an ideal image that looks mighty like a form.

And I am convinced that within the individual is a "sense of injustice," as the legal scholar Edmund Kahn called it, a deep, visceral outrage at arbitrariness or disproportion that we have before we have any rationalized theory of justice, before we have formulated abstract principles or know what is appropriate in different spheres of life.[6]

These are simply some of my personal experiences with what I believe is the power within, the capabilities that we use to justify individual freedom in our deeper philosophy. I believe such experiences are quite ordinary and prosaic, that something like them happens to everybody (but they are no less mysterious for that). However, our ideas of individual inwardness are hardly consensual, common ground. Many would define the qualities of moral individuality quite differently. Many would associate individual morality with entirely different experiences in their own lives. We normally find the inner life of others unfathomable. And we are often deeply suspicious of the authenticity of what others claim to have found in the sanctity of their spirit. I have no idea of what some people mean by a "personal savior," nor do I know what Quakers mean by the "inner light" or how they know when they are in its presence. Our experiences, and our interpretations of the human spirit, are radically different; often they are mutually incomprehensible. Are we then talking about different aspects or expressions of the same phenomenon? Or are we perhaps talking about entirely different things?

To make matters worse, while this ideal of individual inwardness must be one of the great sustained values of our civilization, today we seem singularly incurious about it. We do not explore or discuss the phenomenon. Rather, we try to explain it away. Our official positivist psychology is interested only in surfaces. It does not want to know what goes on in the "black box." It is, on principle, against investigating "the ghost in the machine."[7]

We have legitimate worries about raising the question of individual inwardness. We will, quite likely, be opening the door to all kinds of crackpots, fanatics, bigots, and slushy sentimentalists. It might be better not to. But we really do need to say *something* collectively, publicly, about this vision of human nature that, as a core value of our liberal political philosophy, may be our strongest common bond.

So what do we intend to teach about the human spirit? As a kind of exercise in triangulation that may help us determine our position, let us consider three great efforts to define what the quality essential to our humanity is. The first is modern, and the focus is on the fuller implications of our capacity to reason. The second is Christian, and the emphasis is on our capacity to love. The third is Aristotelian and works outward from our capacity to discern essential purpose and excellence. Perhaps by examining these ideas, plainly and directly, we may begin to grasp the outline of an answer that responds to our affirmations and our doubts.

MORAL INTUITION AND REASON

Many would say that reason is the power that we must find and cultivate if we are to achieve true individuality and freedom. Like all philosophy born in the Enlightenment, liberalism celebrated reason and made it the key to human distinctiveness.

But what, precisely, do we intend to mean by *reason*? Today the term is apt to connote a certain rigorousness in logic or calculation, the way that we think when we do mathematics, when we proceed algorithmically, like a computer. However, the broader classic sense of the idea of reason included much else: our intimations and intuitions, the cunning ways that we draw inferences, our capacity to represent and subsume under categories, our hunches and hypotheses, all our gropings to make sense of things and to proceed effectively and efficiently in the world.

Perhaps the most dramatic effort to capture this broad idea of reason in the name of liberal freedom was that of Immanuel Kant. Kant is properly the father of the idealist version of liberalism. This is the strong alternative to all forms of skeptical liberalism, all those political theories that insist that we must be rigorously agnostic about taking a public position on the question of how to live.

Kant is indeed a rationalist, but his rationalism is not at all like that of skeptical liberalism, the rationalism of calculated self-interest, or even the reciprocal recognition of rights. In fact, for Kant reason is not what makes the individual unique and sacred in the order of things. That power is "the moral law within." But reason is what guides us to this power, bringing us to an astonished awareness of its presence within us. And, most important, reason can check the validity of our moral judgments, make us sure that we are listening to that voice and not some other. Reason can tell us what to make of our moral intuitions, how to fashion them into discrete principles and positive courses of action. Reason, then, is a discipline, a method, an instrumental practice, that brings us in touch with our moral capacities, controls and corrects them. Reason is, then, a kind of spiritual exercise, akin, you might suppose, to the practices of a religion.

Kant's idealism begins in the realization that we act morally only when we act on the basis of our moral sense or our moral will, when we act for the reason that our action is right and for no other reason. Action to win approval or avoid punishment, action motivated simply by respect for custom or authority, action that is merely prudent, is not, we come to realize, moral action, which is born in our sense of duty alone. When we become aware of this quality of our nature, we see ourselves as we truly are. We are the immanent source of meaning in the world: We are all citizens of a "kingdom of ends." Whatever becomes of goodness in the world is, quite practically, up to us, and that too, we now understand, must be the essence of our politics.[8]

How, then, would Kant have us check our intuitions of right and wrong? The process begins in a frank examination of our reasons for action, of the nature of "the maxim of our choice." (Personally, I find this a useful exercise. Before an important decision I sometimes ask myself why I am about to decide in a certain way. I listen to the answer that emerges. The results are often humiliating, a skein of spurious reasoning, concealed self-serving, simple conventionality, and the like. Sometimes, aghast, I do decide to correct my judgment in the light of principle.)

The crucial test of moral action for Kant is, of course, whether you are willing to uphold the principle of your choice consistently, in all relevantly similar situations. This is, practically, what the categorical imperative is all about. Could we "will the maxim of our action to be a universal rule"?

Some argue that the categorical imperative is not a helpful guide to moral action at all. The simple test of consistency can yield trivial prescriptions ("never eat oysters on Thursdays") or horrifying ones ("always kill inferior races").[9] The method can yield appallingly opaque abstract propositions ("Treat humanity, whether others or in your own person, never as a means only, but always as a member of a kingdom of ends") that seem to provide very little help in the hard cases.

However, Kantian method may be the very essence of applied liberalism, and, as we learn the terms of political discourse of our society, we come to know it and use it quite unself-consciously. Liberalism is, above all else, a philosophy of resistance to tyranny, and tyranny implies authority that is arbitrary, whimsical, or self-serving. For the free life to be possible individuals must live and plan in a space that is rationally structured, through institutions and laws that are reliable and comprehensible. This implies that we will base our public decisions on general principles consistently applied. The alternative is Franz Kafka's terrifying world of leaders whose purposes are unknown, courts that cannot tell you why you are being held, and authorities that never speak.

As Philip Selznick remarked, liberalism has a "strain toward consistency."[10] A society based on liberty and equality must find departures from these norms disturbing and perplexing. They must either give good reasons for inequalities or restraints or change them. This is, I truly believe, the persistent pattern of all our political argument. It is the signature of political deliberation in a liberal regime.

John Rawls, I believe, has described most helpfully in his theory of reflective equilibrium how to put into practice this element of Kantian consistency that underlies our liberalism. Start from some strong moral conviction that you already hold, perhaps that racial discrimination is wrong. Now ask what the maxim of your conviction is, the principle on which it is based. Perhaps you will find that you believe deeply that people should not be judged on the basis of accidental or inherent characteristics, qualities they can do nothing about. People should be judged only on acts of their freedom, acts of will, initiative, performance, you now say. Can you uphold this rule consistently? If you would not discriminate on the ground of race, then certainly you cannot on the basis of gender, either. What else? Disability certainly seems to fit. But what about ability? Intelligence and talent are inborn qualities. Is it fair, then, to reward or honor those with exceptional abilities?[11] When we face such an apparent contradiction between our principles and our moral intuition, we recognize that we will have to revise either our principle or our intuition. But something clearly tells us that we cannot just persist in the contradiction. That, it would seem, is simply an imperative of our moral nature, and we presume that it is universal in humanity.

Granted, we can now debate whether what we should or do treat unequally is the talent or the effort invested in developing the talent. But the basic point should be clear. Our liberal beliefs compel us to examine this quandary, and our method of examining it is Kantian.

Critics are fond of saying that you cannot demonstrate any irrefutable moral truths by Kant's method. You cannot prove that slavery is wrong and benevolence is right. This said, they are willing to dismiss the whole enterprise. Again, I think this criticism misses the point of the theory. Especially in the context of liberalism, Kant's method is more akin to a spiritual exercise, a way of making us aware of the inadequacy of our everyday grounds for choice, and of the power within us that acknowledges that this is so, and gives us the ability to correct our actions.

Is this what we should teach coming generations about the quality that justifies our belief in individuality and freedom? My own position, it should be clear, is that Kantian rationalism has a practical place in our teachings. But I do not believe that this says everything we need to say about the power of the individual. I would not subscribe to a public philosophy that was doctrinally Kantian, that adopted Kant's philosophy exclusively as the basis of the regime. I think we would find such a teaching confining and incomplete. We would quickly realize that it has left out too many expressions of what we value in the human spirit. Where, then, should we next turn?

LOVE AND REASON

Another quality has long been thought to capture the essence of our humanity. That is love.

Greek has four words for love. *Eros* is sensual passion, not simply sex but the full force of desire. *Philia* is deep friendship, a true, committed sharing of life's concerns and interests. *Storgi* is the natural affection of parents for children. But the word for selfless love is *agapé*. The early Christians regarded this idea of love as distinct from and greater than the rest.

(Some might suggest that the Latin word *caritas* better captures the sense of love as a practical concern for others and that this seems closer to our concern for the development of a morality of everyday life. But I want to invoke the strongest term that our tradition gives us for the power within that gives the individual moral worth.)

Like so many of the rich Greek words, *agapé* is hard to define simply and surely. I have learned (for I am far from sure that I understand the matter) that it means something like universal and unconditional acceptance, of self, others, all life, and of the world. It implies joy. It means confidence, a belief that the forces behind the universe are benign. In Christian thought love for others comes as a response to grace, to the realization that God accepts us. I do not believe that this awareness is simply a religious matter or a state of the sentiments. I believe that a scientist must know something like this to believe that it makes sense to search for meaningful order in the world.

Yet having said all that, I am not sure that I actually understand *agapé*. The ideal is elusive. Could you actually identify its presence or absence? Writers have described it in countless different ways through the ages. Is *agapé* a rare phenomenon, or is it quite common? Some think it a blessed state of grace that belongs only to the saints. But I can also think of it as a kind of unremarkable openness and generosity of spirit that I witness all the time, in all kinds of people.

Is *agapé* a steady state of spirit, or is it like a sudden epiphany, a tidal wave of awareness, that then leaves you, in quite ordinary states of mind, to recalibrate the direction of your life?

Traditional Christianity teaches that we cannot realize *agapé* fully. Our passions and our interests are inevitably stronger than our will to live truly. Technically, this is what Christian doctrine means by sin. Like the Platonic forms, like Aristotelian telos, like all those intimations that give individual life direction, something about *agapé* will inevitably elude our grasp. And this fact, again, all our philosophy teaches, helps define our essential nature. We are the creatures who are aware that we cannot achieve our own perfection.

What, then, shall we tell the young about this power? What should be our public philosophy of love, and what should we say of the relation between love and reason?

Remarkably, we think that the cultivation of the powers of reason is a proper public responsibility but that we should leave the cultivation of the power of love to the churches. What can we conceivably have in mind? How can these powers be separated?

We express our care and concern for others through our competence. Love is not just a sentiment. It implies effective, careful, intelligent action on their behalf. Skill is the expression of our love.

The mind has a vital role to play in love. We can teach empathy. Through literature or politics we can show the young how to take the point of view of others.

But sheer rational method is sterile, potentially brutal, without a deep consistent concern for those who will be affected by it. Those who would teach us compassion and those who would teach us technique simply cannot work in isolated compartments.

Can a person learn to love? How would you teach it?

The ordinary Christians of the churches, who tend to speak of *agapé* quite casually, at their best seem to mean by it an extension of the natural sentiments that we feel for partners, in friendship and fellowship, to all those who lie beyond the bonds of closeness, and particularly the poor, the despised, and disdained, and the strangers. This is, I believe, a great and simple teaching. Surely, *agapé* is not an idea confined to Christianity. Would not others, Jews, Moslems, recognize it under other names? *Agapé* can be taught through example, by simple acts of kindness. And when we realize that we cannot universalize this ideal, we become aware, again, of the limits of our nature. But why should this be thought a "religious" teaching? Why should we not call it secular or even rational? Is this not an idea of love that most citizens would gladly teach?

Is *agapé* the power that justifies individual freedom? Should we teach that to live truly we must renounce the vanity of the world and follow the deepest urgings of our spirit, a spirit that also is the power that gives meaning to the world? Jesus of Nazareth certainly thought so, and in counseling that we "not be conformed to the world," he affirmed an ideal of individual transcendence that had much in common with the teachings of the Roman Stoics, the Essenes, and other schools of the day. All these are among the direct ancestors of our own liberal individualism.

Should we teach, then, that *agapé* is simply part of our inner nature, that it is an aspect of our reason, intuition, planning, art, and wonder at the world, that these things cannot be separated but must be seen whole? Can we agree that simply assigning reason to the secular realm and love to the sacred is hardly logical?

I believe that love as *agapé* is a necessary part of our public philosophy of liberal democracy and must be part of our common teaching. But that said, we have to be very careful, for we can easily do more harm than good.

The teaching of love as *agapé* is not something that we can legislate. We must not try to define it or set standards for the qualities that we are trying to promote. We must recognize that love is mainly a private matter, between individuals and between ourselves and God. We must understand the wisdom of leaving the ineffable ineffable.

PRACTICAL REASON

All the great Greek words try to capture powers that lie just at the edge of our consciousness. Love as *agapé,* like the Platonic forms, *logos* as the underlying order of the world, and *telos* as the proper end or purpose of the things of the world—all these suggest possibilities of the mind that can direct our efforts and inspire us, even as they elude us. They intimate qualities of reality, invisible underlying appearances that we can never quite grasp. These words speak to our aspirations, not our certainties. In the spectrum of human capabilities they are at the opposite end from—but no more mysterious than—our ability to count, to distinguish colors, to follow a rule.

Aretē is, I believe, one of the most helpful of these evocative terms. Depending on how you use it, its overtones include the ideas of purpose, excellence, rightness, proportion, justice, and perfection. *Aretē* is the key to Aristotle's philosophy, and much of Plato's, and its stunning implications come down to us from these sources.

Everything about the idea of *aretē* implies the capacity of the individual to penetrate beyond convention, to get behind outward appearances. It denotes our capacity to criticize an existing work, a practice, or understanding and to judge that it is not quite right, not yet finished or final, but that it could be improved or perfected so as to better do its job. This capacity is key to our creativity, individuality, notions of skill, and morality. Its mysterious presence is what renders any determinism suspect.

Aristotle taught that trying to understand the meaning of the world, which is to say, its point and purposes, is natural for us. We are not inclined to accept the idea that all is chance and contingency, sheer randomness. Thus we search for an order and direction underlying apparent transitoriness and flux. We ask questions of cause and effect. How did things become this way? What will happen next? How will it all end?

To ask questions of essential end or purpose (telos) cuts through appearances to intrinsic nature. The questions unify the realms of knowledge. Just as we can assert that the natural purpose, the "perfection," of the seed is to become a tree, so we can inquire about the natural purpose, the perfection, of the family, university, church, or state.

The quest to understand perfection, the urge to find out where the world is tending, given the obvious incompleteness and clearly flawed nature of its present state, is the peculiar human inkling that lies behind our search for ultimate meaning. But this is also the power behind our practical reason, our capacity to criticize and try to perfect an existing work. Again, if we were purely creatures of culture, we could not see beyond our established ways of doing things. When we ask truly ultimate questions about the aims of medicine or education or police work, we may open the door to philosophic reflection and the reconsideration of technique. (Is the aim of medicine simply the prolongation of life? Is the aim of education simply the socialization of the young?)

This power lies behind all our everyday creative activities. It is the basis of our skill. Incredibly, we imagine something—and then we make it. And in our work, in the sustained critical effort of making, we both sharpen the image in our minds and the shape of the artifact. This is the power that leads us to take pains. It leads us to try to perfect our performance in every realm. It applies with equal force to the design of aircraft, the writing of books, the development of scientific theories, and the teaching of children. That we are so nonchalant about this power, that we take it so much for granted, is astonishing.

Thinking this way about purpose and excellence generates a very different view of morality. In our times the words *morality* and *ethics* have taken on a distinctly puritanical cast. They seem to have only to do with stricture, with thou shall and thou shall not.

(The microbiologist Lewis Thomas wrote somewhere that in medical school he got the distinct impression that ethics had to do with money and morality had to do with sex, and that was about the end of it.) Morality seems to us a very grim business. And the word *virtue* sounds to our ears distinctly prissy.

But the idea of morality that Aristotle taught is quite different. He links the idea of virtue to practical reason and good performance. Skillful, competent, careful action, action that works toward the perfection of an undertaking, is moral. Shoddiness, carelessness, indifference, and corruption are not.

The virtues, then, are qualities of character and temperament that seem essential to excellence in various human callings. Integrity, conscientiousness, scrupulousness, and painstaking care would seem pertinent to any human activity. But courage, imagination, decisiveness, the capacity for close observation, or the suspension of judgment may be desiderata that pertain to particular vocations or tasks.

Thinking this way can give us a deeper insight into the reasons behind the strictures of ordinary morality. Morality is not simply the repression of passion in the interest of social peace. It is, rather, the condition of proficiency in the natural and necessary projects of humanity. Adultery, abuse, and neglect obviously diminish the natural purposes of the family, as caring, steadfastness, and fairness enhance it. Greed and envy, lust and malice are wrong because they display self-love against *agapé*, passion over reason. But they are also wrong because they undermine the quest for excellence.

The moral philosopher Alasdair MacIntyre argues that we have lost our sense for this larger classical morality.[12] Our modern skepticism leaves us with a morality of crude rules and commandments that we can accept either as the absolute will of God or for reasons of sheer social convention. Thus our moral arguments become undiscussible and undecidable. We can appeal to no shared moral philosophy. Is abortion murder or a matter of individual discretion? Is it good to restrain the passions, or is it wrong to repress our natural instincts? We do not know how to resolve such quandaries. Positivist science tells us that values have no objective referent, unlike facts. Thus, our philosophers argue, our moral vocabulary is no more than an expression of opinion. We admire honesty. We have no taste for greed. Morality is a matter of taste, and that's the end of it.

Unlike MacIntyre, I do not believe that we have lost our capacity for classical moral reason. We can perfectly well grasp the concept and the power of the ancient idea of practical reason. Once it is explained to us, we can use it in our quest for the good. We can understand how this ideal is linked to morality. All we have lost by our learned obedience to the strictures of positivism, utilitarianism, and the like is our awareness of the underlying philosophy. But that we can recapture.

But the point, of course, is not simply to reaffirm ancient virtue. It is to restore our confidence in the idea of liberal democracy, to get to the deeper, surer grounds of our belief in individual freedom.

We cannot teach the realms of the human spirit in separate compartments. Our search, through reason, to be consistent and intelligible blends seamlessly with our efforts to discern purpose and achieve excellence. And all such efforts presuppose that we care endlessly and fully about life and the world and one another. Quite obviously, exercising the powers within takes the form of a quest. These powers serve us as the mountaineer's rope or the miner's pick. They are tools of the inquiring mind. And we know the quest is unending.

THE ELUSIVE IDEAL, DIVERSITY, AND FREEDOM

This is what comes from trying to pin down the essence of the human spirit. For something is always elusive about the qualities that we hope to find and cause to flourish within the individual, something just beyond our grasp. Even the great formulations of our philosophy and religion fail to capture it very well. They reveal at best an aspect, a manifestation, of the quality that we seek. And this is, I hope we can agree, all to the good. For it means that we have no right to establish a particular conception of this power as doctrine, to teach it to one and all as the sole source of knowledge, as the only right way to live. To reduce humanity to one dimension produces a caricature.

Thus we return to liberal openness. But this does not draw us back to relativist liberalism, to the skeptical doctrine that we can affirm nothing about the human good. For now we know the direction of our quest. The whole point is to draw forth and make to flourish all those powers of the mind and spirit that set us apart in the order of creation, that represent the essence of our humanity.

The object is not to bound the expression of the human spirit. And now we realize that this is precisely what raw market liberalism does when it teaches conformity to an ethic of sheer consumer satisfaction and worthiness as material success won through economic competition.

We can again affirm a liberal faith in absolute freedom of expression but now not on the subjectivist ground that all utterances are simply emotional preferences and therefore all count just the same. Rather, we are exploring the diverse possibilities of the mind and spirit, knowing that we have no right to define arbitrarily the proper modes of their expression.

This is a defense of religious and philosophical pluralism but not on the minimalist liberal ground that such tolerance is simply a requisite of social peace. This is a more substantive affirmation of diversity, on the ground that we can awaken individual reason and conscience and develop them in different ways, that each of us is apt to find meaningful different teachings on ultimate matters.

Thus liberal idealism shares the conservative's respect for tradition, for that is where we must begin in finding the meaning of ourselves and of the world. But liberal idealism does insist that our quest not be confined to tradition, for we might very well discover new philosophies, new insights into the human situation.

Liberal idealism teaches tolerance for diverse perspective. But its tolerance is not uncritical. The discourse does not end, as it does so often in liberal emotivism, with the conclusion, "Well, you have your point of view and I have mine." Rather, diverse teachings are mutually criticized in light of the point of the venture, which is to make the most of the potentialities of each individual, to promote individual autonomy, as efficiently and as fully as possible.

So we must engage in public moral deliberation. But are ordinary people likely to participate in such a deliberation? The danger in encouraging any kind of public moral discourse is that it brings out the bigots and the sanctimonious true believers, the righteous fanatics. Let me grant that the great virtue of skeptical liberalism, in its refusal to even talk about the merits of different moralities, is that it thus offers categoric opposition to the party of intolerant meanness. But this may be too high a price to pay. To structure the argument so that the only alternatives are priggish moralism or relativist "anything goes" licentiousness does not seem to be the most intelligent way to proceed.

Our admission that we cannot capture in a single doctrine the qualities that give individuals such extraordinary value does not, as we now see, return us to relativist liberalism. But it does raise the practical question of how we intend to construct our teachings so that the next generations can find these capacities in themselves. How are they supposed to apply these intimations of ideals to the conduct of everyday life?

INDIVIDUAL DISTINCTIVENESS

The first reason for not restricting our idea of essential human nature to a specific set of qualities, to a doctrine, is that we recognize that such a definition would be incomplete. The human essence is, in the end, elusive, inexpressible. We delimit or define it at our peril.

But the second reason for stopping short of clarity, of precise specification in this matter, is that the qualities that we seek are expressed differently in each and every individual. Furthermore, we only encounter these qualities as discrete individuals, with all their quirkiness and defects, express them. We can only know the universal through its distinctly idiosyncratic individual manifestations.

The particular is as elusive as the universal. Each of us finds the others, in all their complexity, bewildering. We try to characterize them. We make an effort to understand them, to size them up. But we recognize that our assessments are uncertain hypotheses, often wild guesses.

Now we have to reckon with individual diversity. The powers that we seek develop differently in each individual. They are expressed in an unruly hodgepodge of temperament and talent.

Some are smart. Some are slow. Some are generous and outgoing. Some are reserved, shy, and solitary. Some grasp the big picture. Some are meticulous about details. Some are hedgehogs. Some are foxes. Some are tough-minded. Some are tender. Some are acutely attuned to the loveliness of the world. Others are tone deaf and oblivious to other degrees of beauty.

Are some of these expressions of the human spirit finer than others? Now we hesitate. We recognize that certain temperaments seem closer to our ideals of excellence, maturity, integrity, or love. We celebrate the great creative individuals and associate their achievements with what is special within humanity. But we also recognize, in the complex mixture of nature and nurture, that none of us is personally responsible for such attributes. We really cannot help being who we are. And we recognize that the distribution of initial endowments in the world is manifestly unfair, a cruel joke. Indeed, many have suggested, the whole object of liberal politics may be to try to overcome the disparities between those who nature has favored and those who nature has deprived and diminished, left out.[13]

We now see anew the significance of our commitment to the liberal principle that all individuals are equally worthy by virtue of their capacity for autonomous action, action not determined by the provisionalities of culture or tradition.

Were we, the elders, to teach this principle in full seriousness, we would first have to learn how to detach ourselves from all the socially convenient conventions that we have learned for assessing individual merit, rewarding the intelligent, the talented, the facile, the dominant, ignoring the ordinary, despising those who cannot quite keep up. We shall have to learn to be openly contemptuous of the superficial grounds on which our culture bestows celebrity and the emptiness of what our media suppose, erroneously, to be charisma.

But do we actually believe, against all convention, against all evidence, that individuals, in all their diversity, are equally worthy? Do we actually think we can discern the workings of the soul behind appearances, beneath vast differences in ability and character? Can we teach each individual, in stark particularity, how to discover and develop those distinctive personal qualities? This is not an idle question. Each parent must answer this question on behalf of each child. So must every teacher. If we fail to do this, if we treat the blessed and the disdained only by socially convenient standards, we lose all integrity.

We know we dare not prescribe in detail how another should live. We must not single out specific traits and temperaments and insist that anyone who matters will exhibit them. Is it not true that what we should do is point to all the intimations of the qualities that I have been discussing here, encourage and suggest, give examples and set situations where these human possibilities might become manifest, and hope that the young will catch on, that they will learn to lead a life guided, as best they can, by the promptings of the spirit?

We have known all along that we cannot teach another how to live. All individuals must learn that for themselves, through a process of trial and error, through an exploration that only makes sense if it is pursued self-consciously, reflectively, autonomously, in the actual conditions of human freedom.

What are the best conditions under which to pursue this quest? Here the conventional liberal is absolutely certain of the answer.

Only in an open society, with a highly differentiated division of labor, a diverse community and associational life, one that professes a free and pluralistic array of beliefs and philosophies, are individuals, in all their particularity, apt to find their niche. Only a society of personal choice and contract, one based on marketlike arrangements in all spheres of life, can support an ideal of life as an ongoing investigation, a quest to find a personal philosophy and the sources of your soul. A conservative, status-bound society cannot do this. Neither can an hierarchically regimented one.

This answer, I believe, is almost correct. But it is not quite enough. It stays on the surfaces. It is too conventionally correct. Taken just as it is, it leads us back into relativism and a society that takes hedonistic satisfaction as its privileged objective. Liberals must teach much more if they are to take the purpose of individual freedom to be the quest to find your own best self.

VOCATIONS AND VIAS

I would like to secularize and make part of a reconstructed idealist liberal democratic public philosophy two particularly useful teachings of classical Christianity. These are the ideas of vocation, or calling, and *via,* or way. I think the two ideas elegantly express what is involved in helping individuals to find their distinctive place in an open and pluralistic society.

To search for your vocation implies a self-conscious, relentlessly honest probing of your capabilities and limits, a thorough survey of the entire relief map of your character. The search may culminate in the discovery of a particular lifework. Or it may lead to a commitment that you could apply to a number of callings. A sense of vocation is more than simple identification with a profession. It is a crucial part of personal identity. I *am* teacher, artisan, public servant, parent. It was intended that I be such. This is my place in the scheme of things. A sense of vocation gives meaning and significance to work. It generates a philosophy of work.

The sense of vocation takes form in relation to the ideals of *aretē,* practical reason, and essential purpose. Finding your vocation means to live according to its inner ethic. Your character and the work become as one. Your aim is to perfect your performance in the light of the standards of the calling. You are entitled to examine its practices and perfect them if you can.

Teaching the young to seek a sense of vocation should offer some protection against social striving and anxiety, frustration and envy. Your efforts are directed more toward the intrinsic goals of the calling rather than extrinsic ends, say, wealth or fame. If your talents are right for the job, that is sufficient. You need not regret not taking part in things that lie beyond your powers.

The classic idea of vocation was subtly egalitarian. True, some callings represented a higher expression of human capabilities, in an Aristotelian sense. But all callings were equally worthy in the eyes of God. Some are called to lives of prayer or philosophy. Some are called to build, maintain, nurture, or protect. In the larger scheme of things each has important work to do. Excellence in the sense of *aretē* is the common measure of achievement and worthiness. This is, of course, a far deeper egalitarianism than the current view, that those who contrive best to sell their talents to the highest bidder are entitled to the richest reward.

To teach the idea of vocation as part of the public philosophy is a way to affirm individual distinctiveness as well as individual autonomy. It is a way to make our idea of the philosophic life acutely particular, practical, and down-to-earth. Vocation is a more significant way of relating the individual to the community than utilitarian calculated contract or conservative conformity. It is a way of deepening the liberal public philosophy and making it personal.

The second term that I would like to resurrect from the older Christian tradition is *via*, the idea that because of our individuality, we will travel different paths, follow different teachings, practice different disciplines, as we try to reach a common goal. In its heyday the church taught a strikingly broad array of possibilities, subtly fitted to different temperaments, each expressing a slightly different perspective on the nature of the divine and the mystery of life. Some might follow the *via dolorosa*, others the *via negativa*. Some were meant for diligent inquiry, following the path of the Jesuits and the Dominicans. Others were fitted to solitude and silence, in the manner of the Desert Fathers.

The conception of the via suggests a pluralism of faith and philosophy that seems congenial to liberalism. But I choose this approach for a reason that goes considerably beyond our ordinary, casual, idea of pluralism.

We tend to teach today that if a philosophy does not yield absolute certainty, what you have instead are paradigms and perspectives, frameworks for understanding that are incompatible and incommensurable, for they share no common standards, no common metric, for adjudicating among these frameworks, for deciding which to accept when their teachings conflict.

This seems to be the dominant contemporary route to relativism in philosophy. It is also the source of contemporary culturism, of the view that the teachings of all societies are arbitrary constructs so that the best we can do is immerse the young in the meanings of their own people, acknowledging that others will see things differently and that their views will often seem strange, incomprehensible, perhaps repugnant.

But the idea of the via suggests that diverse perspectives need not be incompatible or mutually exclusive. They may be no more than different paths to a common end or different interpretations that focus on distinct aspects of a common truth. They need not be incompatible or incommensurable. They may very well be complementary, each revealing a different facet of that which we wish to understand. Is this not the way human understanding usually works? Do we ever expect things to add up in just one way?

And this is the way it is in science. Our understanding of the natural order does not need to resolve into a single picture. The molecular, the evolutionary, the organic, and the ecological perspectives of biological theory are different, yet they complement one another, each enhancing our understanding of the whole order of life.

If we do teach that each of us must find our own way, we must repeatedly stress one fact about *all* ways: Each of us is limited and partial. We are bound to miss much. Thus, while the search for individuality requires a certain inwardness, keeping an eye on the others is worthwhile. They are bound to discover things that we, absorbed in our autonomy, are likely to ignore.

Perhaps some do find "themselves" through a retreat within, in solitude. But I do not think that this is the normal way or the model way. Each of us is, in essence, askew, a strange and somewhat contorted representation of humanity. This is true even of the essential, universal human qualities. We all express them differently. Some are better at love, others at reason. We all have our peculiar talents. But we all are also totally inept at some things that we have to know or do in order to live well. So the others must teach us. Or they may have to do things for us. So we do need to rely on one another. You can become an individual only in a community.

The disdain of the Stoic, or of Thoreau, for society was not misplaced. But what they had in mind was the mindless banality of convention, of popular culture, that can render any of us numb and witless, unseeing. Yet all this is a totally different matter from all the truly remarkable things that we will find other people doing and thinking, seeing and understanding, if we just pay attention, if we just look around.

6

On Human Frailty and
the Problem of Evil

What do we intend to teach the young about the iniquity and sordidness they will face in the course of their lives? They will, of course, be deceived and betrayed. They will be taunted, perhaps ostracized. They will be told they are unworthy, that they do not measure up. They will be ignored and excluded.

And this is only if they are lucky. They may be killed, maimed, or raped. They may be forced into exile. (About one of every 130 people in the world today is a refugee.) They may meet with misfortune—poverty, loneliness, disability—about which no one seems to care. They may find enemies who will twist their words, accuse them of deceit or depravity, and lead them into humiliation.

What shall we tell them about that part of humanity that always finds a way to place itself above the common lot and views the rest with indifference, if not disdain, or prides itself on its ability to manipulate the innocent and the ordinary so that they serve—and admire—the better-off?

What shall we tell them about the inevitability that they too will betray and lie? What shall we tell them about the accident of birth—that if they are born fortunate, they will be most unlikely to give up their privileges and that they will probably rationalize them as just deserts?

What shall we tell them about the fact that we are all going to die?

What indeed do we intend to teach them about the problem of evil?

Of course, the problem of evil really is a problem about the universe. It is a question about God. What, indeed, are we to make of the intentions of the Creator? Christians, particularly, among the religious of the world, tend to think well of their God. Christians have a long tradition, a fusion of the ideas of Athens and Jerusalem, that God is perfect goodness. Christianity teaches that God has our best interests at heart. And this raises some obvious questions: why death? why disease? why calamity? why carnivorousness?

Our official material reductionist science answers that the world is meaningless, the product of random accident. Thus evil is no more or less than pure dumb chance. But this teaching is not a finding of science; no evidence can be adduced for it. Scientific materialism is no more than a methodological precept, a working rule. When science broke with Aristotle in the 1500s, it excluded arguments from design on principle, for they could not be tested by direct observation. Thus we could not even ask if the order of things has a point or purpose. Discussing the problem of whether and how the world, as it is, made sense was out of order. The working postulate was that the world was dumb matter and motion: It did not have a meaning. Today some scientists teach as though they had proved that the universe works by random accident, but they are not entitled to do this. You cannot refute an alternative explanation simply by excluding it from consideration.[1]

Today arguments from intelligent design are back in fashion, even among scientists with no particular religious ax to grind. It turns out that many remarkable things we have so recently learned about the beginnings of the cosmos, the origins of life, or the intimate details of the life of the cell are very hard to explain on the basis of pure Darwinian random mutation and natural selection.

The chemistry of functional proteins is incredibly complex. Serious scientists find it implausible that such structures could evolve by gradual random mutations. Sir Frederick Hoyle, a biologist, said that the chances of DNA's emerging by accident were like "seeing a 747 assembled by a tornado whirring through a junkyard."[2]

The views that life began by accident and that it is the product of design are both utterly fantastic. But neither seems more "scientific" any more. Science, it now seems, must begin in an act of faith. Either you assume that nothing of importance is going on in the universe or you assume that something big is.

But if evil is not simply the product of blind evolution, the problem becomes even more unfathomable. For if there was a designer, what on earth could she or he have had in mind? You and I could design a more acceptable universe in an afternoon. I know our religious traditions counsel faith that all is for the best. But I, for one, think it neither irreligious nor impertinent to believe that we might be entitled to an explanation.

Also, for all the iniquity and imperfection of the world, we the people are still surprised by evil, affronted by evil, perplexed by its presence in us and in the world. Take the position, just for this minute, that the world is a big dumb accident. Why, then, should we be astonished at anything? Why should we feel betrayed by evil, as clearly we are? Why should we expect anything better?

Evil still seems to us an exception to some rule. Killer tornadoes, ethnic slaughter, random shootings, and birth defects still come to us as a shock. We expect order and predictability and even—dare we say it?—goodness and civility.

Another problem is hope. Despair ought to be, but is not, the normal human condition. After the hurricane, after the flood, watch the energy with which people rebuild. Before long they are able to smile and laugh. How do we do this?

Our conception of tragedy must arise from our idealism. The failure of events to live up to some imagined perfection is what leads to disappointment. It would seem that such a sense would lead to a philosophy of futility and despair. The great teachers of idealism in our traditions of thought and religion recognized this and taught something more subtle, that the fact that nothing ever seems to come out just right is evidence not of futility but is a major source of our hope. Our awareness of the gap between our idea of the good and the way that things are is a matter of the greatest significance.

To take the problem of evil seriously, I believe you have to be an idealist of some kind. You have to believe that we are capable of comparing the realm that we live in with a better realm, if we are to suspect the world is not in order as it is. For relativists and materialists, I suspect, evil must seem an imagined problem, a throwback to quaint and out-of-date distinctions of essence and substance, mind and body, the City of God and the City of Man. Once we recognize that the ideal realm is whimsy, the problem goes away. What is left is to accept our finitude, with resignation and irony, perhaps, or with Nietzschean joy and exuberance. Or perhaps we simply talk about evil sociobiologically and discuss the instincts that we have to repress if we are not to commit mayhem.

For pure skeptical liberalism the thin residue of what we might call evil appears mainly as transgressions of rights. To do wrong is to do harm, to violate the conditions of contract or to cause markets to fail.

In pure relativist conservatism evil must be a sort of self-indulgent defiance of the morality of the clan.

But liberal idealism must teach a more classic conception of evil. It must draw on our longer traditions of religion and of thought. It must appeal to the findings of our faith. It must view evil as some kind of failure on our part to do good, or some kind of limitation on our ability to do good, that is rooted in our finitude.

THE PUBLIC PROBLEM OF EVIL

We are, as a nation, deeply divided on the problem of evil, and the politics of this issue do not seem superficial. The antagonists have apparent abiding contempt for one another. This looks like a fundamental rift in philosophy and psychology. In our society it is also something of a predictable set piece. The argument has become a cliché, which is too bad, because the argument has consequences, and they are serious.

Basically, those who tend to call themselves conservatives seem to believe that liberals teach a permissiveness and licentiousness that must be rooted either in total naïveté or else in complete lack of scruple. What else can they believe from what they see and hear but that liberals actually endorse the promiscuity, ridicule, and contempt for all forms of authority and decency that they see all around them?

For their part those who tend to call themselves liberals tend to think that conservatives are rigid and puritanical, obsessed with infraction and depravity, compulsive to punish without understanding or mercy. The liberal seems to suspect that malice, hypocrisy, cruelty, fear, and perhaps barely concealed envy must underlie this fanaticism.

The contrast is extreme—but these are not straw figures. We have met these people. They are familiar. Perhaps our nature is simply to dwell either on human possibilities or human depravity. Still, the question necessarily arises: What could we teach, then, that would be recognizably more intelligent than raw permissiveness or raw repression?

THE LIBERAL THEORY OF EVIL

Liberalism has always seemed an optimistic philosophy, a lasting legacy of the sweet reasonableness of the Enlightenment. Antiliberals of all stripes (say, from Joseph-Marie de Maistre, the seventeenth-century French polemicist, to Leo Strauss, the twentieth-century U.S. political philosopher) have thought us insufficiently grave, innocent of the real situation.[3] Reinhold Niebuhr called us the irrepressible "children of light," never wary enough of the sinister motives of the "children of darkness."[4]

The image is totally misleading. Liberalism, born in response to the horrors of the wars of religion, has had to confront every form of barbarity that we have inflicted on one another in the modern age. Partly because liberals believed so firmly that individual dignity and mutual respect were right, they had a clear idea of the forms of human conduct that were wrong. And despite their belief in the potential reasonableness of people, liberals could take an utterly realistic view of human depravity. They expected the strong to try to dominate and exploit the weak. They thought that tyranny was not an extreme case but something very likely to occur unless people guarded carefully against it. Liberals assumed that malice and mistrust would surface when people of differing philosophies or customs had to live together in a common space.

They assumed that the community would be divided into "interests," each of which would connive to win advantage over the others, each convinced of its rightfulness, each uncomprehending of the others. Liberalism was perfectly cognizant of all the forms of perversity of the human soul and particularly those with public import—those born in the hatred and contempt for other kinds of people that is the product of pride and self-righteousness or fear and insecurity.

Perhaps the critic thinks innocent the liberal view that these evils are controllable. Liberals believe that political institutions can be contrived that will check and balance interests, forestall tyranny, and prevent dominance and intimidation, both from the state and among private parties. The trick is to create a government of a particular kind, one with clear and limited powers, one whose main charge is to secure individual rights.

Is it naïve of liberals to think that statecraft can control evil? Perhaps. Many liberal regimes have failed, and even the best liberal regimes have their share of corruption, violence, exploitation, and sheer human terror. But liberal constitution making rests on a long tradition of cold-blooded realism. Liberal politics always has rested on a fragile and precarious understanding. All the jealous, contriving, fearful forces and factions must somehow come to their senses and put civil peace above their various ambitions, hostilities, and grievances.[5]

The crucial question remains: Do liberals think that evil can be restrained through politics, or do they think it can be eliminated? At this point we reach a major fork in the river, and we must decide which branch to take.

Classic liberalism tends to think of human nature in steady-state terms. People are pretty much always the same. The classic liberal view of the human situation parallels the Newtonian view of the universe: It is constant and timeless.

Classic liberalism rests on a remarkably straightforward view of human frailty. In the foundation myth, the thought experiment of the social contract, John Locke asks us to assent to two simple, sensible-sounding propositions. Could we not assume that in a hypothetical state of nature, before custom and before law had come to shape our values, that reasonable self-interested people, without memory and without preconception, would just naturally recognize the advantages of peace, cooperation, and goodwill over an unending "war of all against all"? But would it not also be reasonable to assume that, in the state of nature, we would all also recognize that some elements of the community always, and all of us sometimes, might take advantage of others? Therefore would not any reasonable being recognize the convenience of a government to protect us against the total unreasonableness and maliciousness of a few, and the occasional unreasonableness of us all, and to provide an impartial arbiter, because none of us is a good judge when our own interests are at stake?

This is the source of the bare-bones liberal theory of politics and of morality and the problem of evil. We are naturally cooperative, but we will sometimes fall from grace unless we are restrained. This is the human situation. It is universal and it is timeless.

Another view of our condition is associated with the liberal tradition. Here human nature is not a constant. Rather, our strange knowledge that the world is not as it should be enables us to criticize and then to transform ourselves and our circumstances. Astonishingly, by taking thought, we can actually increase the amount of good in the world and diminish the amount of evil.

This liberal vision emerged alongside, and was to some extent inspired by, the evolutionary theories of the cosmos, life, and history that emerged and flourished just over a century ago. In our time these theories have largely displaced the timeless Newtonian view of the universe in the minds of those who try to think about the nature of our whereabouts. However mysteriously, we were now to think of life and all reality as a process. We were going somewhere, though neither the cosmologists nor the biologists nor the political philosophers could quite say where we were headed.

Some call the evolutionary version of liberal political theory *perfectionism,* for it takes the task of politics to be not just the maintenance of civil freedom but the enhancement and realization of human capabilities, human flourishing. The term is probably misleading. Granted, Hegel and Marx sometimes spoke in utopian terms, but Mill and Dewey and most of the others did not. The great progressive liberals were very wary about pronouncing on how this was apt to come out.

Obviously, the kind of liberal idealism that I am working toward belongs to the family of progressive thought. Thus we do have to decide what we are to teach about the ultimate aims of our efforts. It is, I believe, always irresponsible to delimit human possibilities. We simply do not know how we might change, biologically or culturally, over the longer reaches of time. Yet I think that implicit in the one core insight on which I have been building since the beginning—that we are the creatures who understand that we do not understand—is that we should not expect to escape our finitude. So cannot we just assume that in the end we will still have a sense of incompleteness, that yearning and sorrow will still be with us?

I also think that we must teach that nothing guarantees that such progress as we make need be permanent. Nothing about anything that we have learned, created, or concluded is necessarily fitted to survive. We could forget both chemistry and the wrongness of slavery. We could collapse, in some totally unexpected way, into barbarism once more.

Still, I believe we can teach a starkly realistic and honest optimism. We know perfectly well that we can create endeavors that bring out the best in ourselves, for we do this all the time. We know that we can use our intelligence to reduce suffering, inhumanity, and danger, for we have done this as well. We know that we can improve the conditions of human freedom, for we have seen this happen, and in our own time. We can, to a totally unknown and unpredictable extent, reduce the burdens of our finitude. But in the end we remain tied to Earth. Our ignorance of our fate shall remain, as shall our fears and our lusts and our envy. And we are all going to die.

My teaching is beginning to sound remarkably Augustinian. I would recognize, as so much of our philosophy and religion has recognized, that we are at once transcendent and finite. We are mind and body, essence and accident. Thus our labor is inevitably the labor of Sisyphus.

Is this a matter on which we might actually agree to a common teaching? Many will doubt it. Given the rivalry of the creeds, secular and sacred, there would seem to be little chance of anything like a working public agreement on ultimate questions. But how much variance is there, really, in the way that we understand our situation? How many really would be willing to declare with absolute confidence that through things like genetic engineering and space colonization we can overcome our finitude? How many, on the other side, are convinced beyond every doubt that we are no more than a random species wandering our way to extinction? How many who live by strong scriptural faith think our yearning will be resolved before the coming of the Kingdom? Just how many, really, would be willing to say that absolutely nothing about our being here is mysterious?

Granted, we all want to frame the story in our own way, and we all have our own hunches, guesses, and fears. But is it not possible to say, at least, that we all know that there is a problem about the world and that we are the ones who perceive it?

MORAL EDUCATION

Today we are deeply divided by what to teach the young about right and wrong. This is a raw sore in our politics. We pick at it constantly.

Conservatives, it seems, would teach an ethic that focuses on personal responsibility and respect for authority. What is important is hard work, paying your own way, conscientiousness, seriousness, faithfulness. What is wrong is dependency—whether on the state, drugs, or others—idleness, whiny or sarcastic alienation, promiscuity.

The cultural left, it appears, is most concerned to teach a morality of tolerance and respect for difference. What is right is to draw in those who have been left out. What is wrong is bigotry, self-righteousness, cliquishness, failures of empathy.

I have no bone to pick with either of these moral urgings. I think that teaching good manners and basic self-discipline is right. I believe that our half-ignored, half-indulged, carefully isolated children of ordinary privilege have to learn to understand and live with the rest of the world. I believe the same applies to those who grow up in a barrio or a ghetto.

Moral education begins in early childhood in the simple inculcation of good habits. But those who want their children to live in freedom have the subtle task of giving direction to these efforts. We think that the moral development of the child begins in fear of punishment, passes into the desire to please, and culminates, if all goes well, in an eagerness to do the right thing for its own sake. We think that parents who are either too permissive or too authoritarian can thwart this process. The trick seems to be to set clear limits and guidelines and give reasons for them. The aim is to nurture moral autonomy, to develop the power to make judgments of better and worse. But all the conventional wisdom of moral education leads up to the awakening of this capacity. But when the young are at last ready, how should we go on? How is this capacity for moral judgment best cultivated and perfected? What indeed do we intend to teach about the distinction and presence of good and evil, how not to confuse them in the twilight cases, how to deal with the subtle instances where they seem to meld into one another, or where the path to evil seems inescapable?

Again, I would teach that a deep, absolute evil is locked into the nature of the world. We know this evil through our strange sense that something is wrong with the world, that it could be better. This is the evil that we can do nothing about.

But another kind of evil is the result of human actions. This evil is an error of some kind. It is a failure to do good. This evil we can do something about.

Let us start from the homely observation that people do not set out to do evil. Rather, they misconceive the good. How does this happen?

Of course, we have discussed this matter in all sorts of ways for centuries. But consistent with our interest in the individual's moral capacity, I think we can boil the matter down to two straightforward types that bear close examination.

First is the failure that occurs when we get so caught up in custom and convention, in the expectations of our tribe or our calling, that we fail to achieve the detachment necessary to exercise moral judgment. Second is the failure that occurs when we are convinced that our individual moral judgment is absolutely and necessarily right, and all the rest are wrong.

Other evils follow from a failure of perspective, of detachment. We accept (and many tell us that we should) a conventional ethic and its virtues. We do not notice when the ethic becomes self-serving or positively destructive.

Usually, philosophers today locate such an ethic in a "culture" or a "tradition." I think this is misleading. Given the amorphous public ethic of our society, the more intense ethical commitment for many of us lies in our professional code. A profession, after all, is only peripherally a body of skill and technique. It is mainly a morality.

The scientist's code of epistemological integrity, of truth telling; the physician's ethic of rational compassion; the military code of courage, duty, and honor—all have this quality. These moralities cut deep. They change lives. Professional education today, I believe, is far more certain than religious conversion. These codes are a primary source of personal philosophy in the contemporary world; they give life meaning. A professional code is in its nature Aristotelian. All teach the virtues of responsibility and efficiency in pursuit of essential purpose. All such codes are practical techniques for making moral action routine. The aim of a professional code is to prefigure crucial choices and give guidance for judgment. But for those who fail to be a bit wary and detached, for those who throw themselves heart and soul into a professional morality, the consequences may be fatal. To become cocooned in such a code is to become morally oblivious. You end up not seeing the forest for the trees.

The edifying example from our time is, of course, Adolf Eichmann. To the end Eichmann seemed to believe that he had done the right thing. He was conscientious, efficient, and thoroughly professional. He had done his duty. He thought that he should not be reviled but commended. But the world that condemned Eichmann—the liberal, relativist, secular world, in fact—in shock and horror, expected him to be conscious of the evil of his acts. That was a morally idealistic world, not a world that believed in the relativity of values or in morals as a social construction. It expected Eichmann to transcend his situation; it expected Eichmann to be autonomous.

Failures of autonomy need not be this dramatic. We are capable of all kinds of everyday sordidness because of excessive commitments to such institutional and professional moralities. We are, all of us, to some extent implicated in the self-righteousness of those who belong to a caste. We commit ourselves to the ways of the corporation, the university, the law, medicine. Equally earnest believers surround us. Perspective vanishes. Looking from the inside out, we fail to see the ways in which we have become ridiculous. Such a state of mind may not lead us to commit acts of terror. Mostly, it leads to lesser barbarities, those of gratuitous insult to those we serve, for example. This is, at least, a steady source of stultification and unconscious humiliation in the world.

Clearly, if we are going to teach the young the kind of individuality that is inherent in liberal idealism, we are going to have to teach them to keep a certain distance from the constructed codes of the world. While we can teach them that these codified ethics can provide great guidance as we try to achieve best practice in a calling, they can never substitute for the moral judgment of the individual. The individual must weigh and appraise the morality of the profession as well as that of the culture.

The first kind of failure of moral judgment comes when we cannot see beyond a conventional code. The second kind comes when we are totally convinced of the rightfulness of our judgment. Blind subservience is a source of evil. So is self-righteousness.

The problem, of course, is that our moral judgment is frail and uncertain. We see, as the New Testament says, through a glass darkly. The "voice within" may be mistaken, or we may not understand it, or we may presume that it has spoken when it has not. Simply to counsel the young to think for themselves and to follow their consciences begins to seem like exceedingly risky, rash advice. Certainly, it is not to have said enough.

We waver. Perhaps we have been mistaken. Perhaps individual moral autonomy, if not exactly a will-o'-the-wisp, is, then, a power far too uncertain for us to put much confidence in it. Perhaps the relativists, the constructionists, and the emotivists have it right. Perhaps we should teach the young not to trust their moral intuitions. Perhaps we should teach them not to trust in autonomy. Let us consider an alternative teaching.

We could return to the older emotivist form of relativism and teach the young that our moral judgments are so uncertain, so apt to be distorted by emotion, disposition, taste, and personal history that they are not to be trusted.[6] We should regard them as no more than our personal "preference," no better or worse than any other person's "opinion." Then we say that reason cannot settle differences on a moral question, for morality has no rational foundation. The best we can do is bargain, compromise, and in the end count heads. Moral questions are really political questions.

Did we come all this way to return to relativism? I think not. We continue in our wonder at the power within individuals to discern essential purposes, to criticize, to evaluate, to look for a better way. All we know is that our initial judgments are not trustworthy, which is equally true of anything else that pops into our heads or that we reason about at length. We need the help of others: We need them to question, to challenge, to study the implications of our initial intimations.

Our inner lives, we know too well, are not to be trusted. Left entirely alone for too long, we lose perspective. We imagine things. We become hurt by trifles. We misunderstand and dwell on our misunderstanding until we seethe with rage. We despair. We become fanatic. Only other people can save us from our madness, can talk us back into the world of common reality. The surest safeguard against the evil that is born of fantasy in each of us is that we are not all apt to go crazy in the same way at precisely the same time.

Even this safeguard, we know perfectly well, is not absolute. We are given to mass hysteria, to mass illusions. This is why it is so important to keep listening to the doubters among us, to those who somehow see through, mistrust, our collective illusions. It is also why it is essential to be true to the way of inquiry, to keep doubting and probing, no matter how sure we are at the moment of the self-evidence, the hard truth, of our illusions.

For others to understand our initial moral conjectures, we are going to have to speak or write about them. We need to make a reasoned case if others are to understand us and grasp what made this view seem more plausible to us than evident alternatives. So we proceed to reason. We make distinctions. We point out similarities. We adduce evidence. We do all the things that are conventional in thinking. And the important point is that going through this process without revising our initial judgment in some important way is virtually impossible. So even before we have addressed the others, our anticipation of this meeting, our very effort to communicate to them what is on our minds, has provided an important check on initial judgment.

Reasoning, like any act of discursive writing, is not a matter of making a case for a predetermined end. Reasoning, like writing, is always an act of exploration. You do not actually know how you are going to come out in the end, and you are usually surprised. Everyone who has ever written an essay knows this. You start from the propositions and distinctions, the metaphors and analogies, that occur to you. But you correct and refine and clarify, gropingly, experimentally but always in the direction of some hint of meaning that you are trying to capture.

In the end you submit your case to the others. Then you listen and respond, as the exploration begins again. And again, if you have integrity, if you are honest, you do not know for sure where you are going to end up at the end of the day.

Shall we teach, then, that the attitude that is appropriate to moral judgment is that of inquiry and that that same attitude is appropriate to science or philosophy or any activity that requires clear reasoning and honest investigation?

Charles Sanders Peirce, the turn of the century philosophic pragmatist, insisted that you do not actually engage in inquiry unless you are trying to learn something, unless you are seeking the truth. If you are already convinced that you know the answer, or if you think that no answer exists, you are not inquiring, you are simply trying to persuade or sounding off or showing off. This means that we should teach that when we enter into deliberation with others, we should regard our initial moral judgment as hypothesis, an idea that needs to be tested. You are prepared to revise it or abandon it, if you become persuaded that it is wrong. Your job is to look for the truth. You are accepting your finitude and the dimness and uncertainty of your vision. You are trying to learn, to do better, with the help of your friends.

Only this attitude is suitable for inquiry in any realm. It implies wariness and a willingness to reconsider your deepest convictions in the name of truth. Everything else is pseudoinquiry. Its practitioners are, in some good measure, frauds. And pseudoinquiry is common in every field of endeavor, in science, in politics, in literature, in philosophy itself.[7]

None of this implies that we should sit around irresolute, weighing and pondering, while the time for action passes and the barbarians are laying waste the fields. Moral action does require that we act on our best guess about the situation at hand, the one for which we are responsible.

You see in all kinds of people a particular disposition—does it have a name?—that first weighs carefully and then acts decisively. It begins in openness and waiting, passivity, taking in without preconception or commitment, and then at just the right moment it acts confidently, basing its action on the best conjecture. You see this very specific and undiscussed disposition all the time in doctors, scientists, pilots, and police. And when it is absent in those who follow such callings, you notice the failure.

If any of this is right, the moral life requires precisely the same aptitudes for reason, inquiry, openness, experiment, and caution that are essential to science, practical reason, and any other kind of intelligent activity in the world. And if this is right, ethics and science are simply different aspects of that one single important human undertaking that we might as well call the search for the truth.

PART III

Relationships

7

Individuality and Relationship

So much is said these days about the social nature of the self, about how we are all socially constituted and historically situated, that it comes as something of a shock when we realize once again, as we must, that every individual is different, that each person is unique.

No two people understand the world in precisely the same way. Imagine the most tightly closed, homogeneous society that you can, unchanging, determined to preserve every nuance of its doctrine, its customs, and its traditions. Do you think that you would find no individuals there? Do you think that everyone would think and act precisely the same?

The fact of individuality can be frightening. It means, after all, that in the end we are destined to live and die alone.[1] We touch each other at only a few points on the surface of our being, a few degrees on the circle of all that we are. The rest of me, the rest of you, remains remote, strange, unreachable. This is perhaps particularly true of friends and lovers. We may be close to unity, to understanding, to actually knowing each other, on this point or that. Here and there we see the world as one. But there are vast tracts, vast depths, where we hardly comprehend each other at all, hardly know the other is there. Often, we are just guessing, and at any moment we may miss the mark and bring about misunderstanding, resentment, heartbreak, loneliness. Intimacy need not mean what it seems to. Anyone who reads seriously knows what it feels like to understand someone you have never met better than you understand those who are closest to you. The secrets that

93

lovers share and keep from the rest of the world are normally quite mundane. We can never close the distance between us. Nor, if the truth were told, do we want to.

Martin Buber: "All true living is meeting."[2] Well, yes, but those moments when we see one another all the way through are rare and fleeting. They are all condensed into a word, a laugh, or a glance. During most of the time that we spend together, we stay on the surfaces—and in the shadows. The moments of encounter may change our lives, we may remember them forever, but they do not take up much time.

Some will tell you that the end of our longing is to be found in reunion with community or with God. But this is not quite so. We do not want to be identical, and we do not want to be extinguished, absorbed into the whole. We desire to preserve our uniqueness. Do you not feel that, when at last you see eye to eye, when you have at last found common ground, your next step is to differentiate yourself in some way? Just to take exception on some small point. Just to move a degree off to another point of view. We cannot stand commonality for long. The differences between us are what interest and attract us. We do not seek perfect unity. We seek complementarity.

We want to keep our secrets, and we want to keep our distance. We tell one another only a minute fraction of what we actually think. We intend, for the most part, not to be understood. We want to be separate, distinct. The writer Robert Fulgum said somewhere that love is like a dance. We take one step forward, then one step back. We want to come closer. And we want to keep our distance.

Rousseau had the truly odd thought that in primitive society, "before art had molded our behavior," people were totally candid and thus totally transparent to one another. Only with civilization did we learn to be opaque. We learned manners, discretion, manipulation. We adopted a persona, a way that we pretended to be. Rousseau thought the ideal society would be one in which people's dispositions would all be known to one another. Then "neither the secret machinations of vice, nor the modesty of virtue could escape the notice and the judgment of the public."[3] But, then, Rousseau, who based his image of humanity on an idealized picture of the life of alpine peasants, had a lot of peculiar ideas about what he imagined rural intimacy to be.

Individuality does not imply solitude. You can be yourself, and keep your distance, in a crowd or in the bosom of community. Individuality does not imply loneliness. You can be totally engrossed with others, totally oblivious to the peculiar fact of your uniqueness and aloneness virtually forever. Individuality is not the same as difference. Some people are sports fans and some homebodies, some ambitious and some easy-going, some habitual entertainers and some withdrawn. But these are simply traits of personality. Lots of other people fit the same category. This is not what makes you an individual, not what is distinctive of you alone. Individuality does not mean eccentricity. Your deviation from some norm is not the measure of your individuality.

In the unending chicken-and-egg controversy about the self, communitarians point out the ways in which our idea of who we are is a social construct, and liberals stress the individual's capacity for choice and judgment. In fact, this is not an argument. Communitarians are not, on the whole, determinists. They know perfectly well that people reinterpret and reconstruct the ideas that are given to them. And liberals know perfectly well that what individuals have to choose and judge about are the artifacts of culture.[4] Where you start from, and what you seem to insist on, depends largely on what you are trying to figure out, and I am trying to figure out how individuals as different from one another as we are can ever come to understand one another as we seem to. If we follow this line of inquiry, I believe, we will see an interesting picture of liberal politics and liberal society emerge, and a number of other perhaps unexpected things as well.

We are irredeemably individuals. We must live within our own souls. We can never quite connect with, far less become one with, another human being. Yet we reach out for one another, desperately. We seek each other for affection, cooperation, sheer survival. We find our meaning in the company of others.

We are, as everyone has said, social animals, but this is not to have said enough. We have a natural affinity for one another, but solidarity is not automatic. Every human relationship has to be separately forged, negotiated and decided, fashioned to fit its particular inhabitants. Every human encounter, however full of hope and anticipation, is also laden with uncertainty and uneasiness; it hangs on the brink of disappointment, perhaps despair.

We reach out to understand and to be understood. But we can only hope to reach another in a small area of common being. All the rest is unknown, transitory, excluded from this relationship. The thought seems sad, forlorn. But in truth, again, we do not want to be completely known or completely understood. We know exactly how much we want to be alone.

This is what most of our philosophy and our literature is about. It is ultimately one of the only things that interests us. We write and speak mainly about the incompleteness of our relationships. Our endless repetitive love stories are mostly about relationships that are never quite requited, that never quite endure. At another level altogether our daily lives, our working lives, are a constant story of missed communication, failed cooperation, screw-ups, as we say.

Other people are, literally, unfathomable. We must view our efforts to understand one another as hypotheses, hunches, guesswork, groping. We must start with the assumption that our first impressions may be totally wrong. We must test our theories about other people through the same process that we would use to find order in nature, find meaning in a difficult text or in an art object. Our hypotheses must always be tentative. We must be ready to revise or reverse them at any time.

We test our initial conjectures about one another through the process of mutual inquiry that is the relationship itself. The process is one of hitting it off, quarreling, making up, explaining, misunderstanding again, apologizing again. At each step the relationship deepens, as we revise and perfect our theory of the other. Otherwise, we go our separate ways. Either way, there is always surprise.

Empathy, then, is not natural sympathy. It is not an emotion. It is a process of finding out. It is imagining yourself in the shoes of the other. It is a matter of shrewd observation and skeptical analysis. Of course, you must also care enough to want to find out.

Naturally, in a true relationship we discover unknown things about ourselves. In this sense, knowing each other is unlike knowing a stable object in the world. I develop through the relationship; my meaning changes, as does yours. We have to keep changing our theories of one another, and of our common bond, as we go along. What we discover is indeed alikeness, identity. Aristotle was right: Friendship requires a shared interest in some good. But the differences deepen the relationship and extend its mystery. Do we really seek someone who agrees with us on every point, who is just like us? The odd angles, the distinct point of view, the thoughts we think bright or funny because they are not ours, sheer quirkiness and whimsicality—these interest us. We are looking for yin and yang, a harmony of differences, or, best of all, complementarity.

To find a good relationship, whether of friendship or love, colleagueship or collaboration, you have to accept the fact, humbly and with gratitude, that somebody else is better than you are at many things that you have always tried to do by yourself alone. Complementarity enlarges the competence of both of you. It enlarges the range of meanings, the significance of your lives. You are now better at map reading, appreciating Bach, supervising, seeing the ridiculous in certain kinds of solemnity. But how the other person knows all the things that you do not remains a mystery. Again, the odd fact is that you know just about as much about the meaning of the person closest to you as you do about the meaning of the universe.

The conservative communitarians do not think that relationship is mysterious. We find one another, they assure us, through the meanings and understandings, the memories and traditions, the practices and roles, of our culture. To be sure, we do get along, day to day, by staying on the surfaces, relating mainly through the quips and courtesies, the assumed opinions and prejudices of "people like us." Still, is relating to another in that way a way of knowing the other at all? The committed communitarian seems to believe that nothing more is there than the socially constructed self. I bet that you do not believe this. Neither do I.

At the extreme, conservative communitarians insist that we cannot understand those who do not share our culture's ways of knowing. Where on earth have they been living? Most of us have friendships that cut across cultural boundaries. A few years back I had an unusually easy and down-to-earth relationship with a student who was a Kazak, Moslem, woman, and a Marxist-Leninist political theorist. (She was taking a crash course with me in liberal democratic political theory, the demand for her specialty having suddenly evaporated.) Literally, it would seem that we came from opposite ends of the earth. Yet we had more in common, and seemed to understand each other better, than I did any of my neighbors at the time, people who were putatively just like me.

We must consider another form of relationship. In our society we work and play together mainly through rationally developed practices and techniques. A special virtue of the people of the modern world is that they analyze virtually every human activity, take it apart, think it through, and put it back together in some standardized way that is supposed to be as efficient as possible in meeting the end in view. We teach these methods to the practitioners. It would seem that we try to reduce individuality in order to instill discipline, to achieve interchangeability of performance so that any properly trained person can carry out a task reliably and well. We do this for flight crews, hotel clerks, surgeons, and soccer goalkeepers.

More than a few of our social critics have lamented this process. They find it dehumanizing, stifling, boring. Max Weber thought of it as "the iron cage." But for most people, performing a task well according to a discipline is enriching and satisfying. Here the fit between the person and the task is all important. You and I might not rejoice at making a living by driving a city bus, but some people love it.

The main point is that associating rational practice only with the mind-numbing monotony of the assembly line or check-out counter distorts our view. Most of our rational practices require imagination and interpretation—sheer art—on the part of the performer. A prime source of human exaltation must be the expression of individuality through a rigorous and subtle discipline.

And most of these rational practices involve relationships with others. This must be the source of some of our most intimate and important encounters. What we seek from one another in these intricately fashioned frameworks of work and play is a special style, a personal grace and competence won through study and concentrated effort. This is what makes for the special bonds that we find in athletics, the performing arts, engineering teams, in military units. Teamwork is one of the most intense ways in which we experience both the vividness of individual distinctiveness and the peculiar intimacy of complementarity. It is, I believe, one of the most revealing forms of our love. We shall have to keep in mind both images, the spontaneity of discovery in a primary relationship and the discovery of one another in the context of rational practice, as we probe the question further. The two overlap, complement, and strengthen one another.

This effort to take stock of ourselves and the bonds between us has four building blocks. We must add two more dimensions to the simple compound of individual and relationship. First then is individuality. Then comes our search for one another in a real relationship. Now we add culture, including rational practice, and that is third. And fourth is our universal humanity. We have talked about how individuals try to find one another. We understand how our conventions and practices give form and purpose to relationships among unique individuals. What now shall we say of the ways in which the universal qualities of humanity bear on our efforts to be alone and yet find one another?

With good reason our classic philosophy teaches that we should be able to share some experiences and understandings, whatever our background, whatever our culture, whatever our point in historical time. Mathematics seems like that. So indeed does parental love. I claim that anyone can see that arbitrary treatment by rulers is unjust. The list can go on and on.

Still, once this is said, the baffling fact is that people seem to vary widely, strangely, in their capacity to appreciate these apparently universal qualities of humanity. Some catch on and some do not. Some are transfixed by music or mathematics, and some are

oblivious to their charms. Everyone should be able to learn a language, but not quite everyone does, and some do better at it than
others. Some traits that we thought were common to our species
seem to lie on some sort of strange continuum, with all sorts of
humps and tails, weird distributions.

So we are back to the mystery of individuality once more. We
are back with the strangeness that we can touch some, but apparently not everyone, with a vision of truth or beauty or fineness or
any of those qualities that we think should be the common mark
of our kind. We are back with the fact that each person represents
universal humanity in one particular way. We are back with the
fact that we can never know others absolutely, to the very depths
of their souls. We are back with the fact that every individual is
unique, which need not be a sad or lonely thought at all, for it is
apparent that, as we cherish our own distinctiveness, so too do we
cherish the distinctiveness of the others.

I dwell on this vision of individuality because I am trying to
develop a better version of liberal political philosophy. Curiously,
the weakest part of conventional liberal theory is precisely its thin,
abstract, atomistic picture of the individual. This is where the enemies of liberalism have always concentrated their fire. Whether in
their Lockean, utilitarian, or Kantian versions, these terribly formal representations of who we are fail to inspire. Conventional
liberal theory has no people, only axioms.

For a third of a century and more we have spent much effort to
teach about diversity, difference, inclusion, and tolerance. But the
emphasis has been almost entirely on group characteristics, specifically, race, class, and gender. Peculiarly little talk has been about
individual diversity and difference. Why is this? Why is the phenomenon of individuality not part of this discussion?

This is why I want to propose a deeper idea of individuality, one
that starts with our uniqueness, moves through our efforts to find
and understand one another, and ends in the realization of our
incompleteness, and thus the finitude, of ourselves and all our relationships. Again, I believe that our ability to recognize our incompleteness tells us much about the kind of creatures that we are.

Now let us see how this picture of individuality deepens, but does not displace, the classic liberal ideal of how relationships and community are properly formed in freedom.

I want to work from the four facts about humanity that I have invoked and the four forms of relationship that go with these facts. The first fact is individuality and the form of relationship that ensures our individual freedom is, in liberal thought, the contract. The second fact is our effort to understand one another, our quest for true relationship, and the form of true relationship is inquiry, but always it is a form of inquiry that presupposes love. The third fact is our socially constructed nature, that we are indeed creatures of culture, and the form of relationship here is convention, custom, role, and rational technique and practice. The fourth fact is our common humanity. The form of relationship that goes with that is our recognition of our universal kinship, our brotherhood, our sisterhood.

Each of these facts and forms creates the idea of human nature that lies at the base of some philosophy. We are, we are told, essentially an individual, an encounter and relationship, a social and cultural construct, or an example of universal humanity. Still, reducing all of our life together to one of these dimensions should, I think, make us uneasy. I do not think that we can live by one of these images alone. I certainly do not think that we ought to try to. So the art and skill of relationship that I would teach is one of taking bearings from these ideas, seeking the points at which they slide together easily and harmoniously, avoiding the extremes, the relationships that fit only one of these dimensions. Like a canoe trip, the object is to veer away from rocks and shoals, to find the current.

INDIVIDUALITY AND CONTRACT

Conventional liberal thought views all relationships not just metaphorically but legally and ethically as forms of contract. The idea of contract comes, of course, from the world of commerce, and we can never quite shake it loose of these associations. This is too bad, for in the longer legacy of liberal thought contract is one of the great general ideas. As a model of association, it replaced all the complex distinctions of status, rank, and function, of privilege, monopoly, and presumption, that marked medieval society. It applied to all associations, not only commerce but religion, community, the university, the guild, and the family as well. It prescribed that all relationships be freely chosen. This is the image against which liberalism measures the rightfulness of all relationships. We applied it to slavery 150 years ago. Today we apply it to gender. I pray that tomorrow we will apply it to certain distinctions of wealth and occupation.

The terms of ideal contract teach a nice straightforward morality. The parties to a contract must be shown to be equals in all significant respects. The formation of the contract cannot involve deception or coercion. The parties must have freedom of choice. All parties must have a roughly equivalent alternative at the outset, and they must be able to leave the relationship for a roughly equivalent alternative at any time. (This is why monopoly is bad and pluralism is good.) There must be no externalities. The costs or benefits of the arrangement must not pass to others unless they are party to the contract, unless they contract in. (This means, of course, not dumping sludge on your neighbor's land. It also means that listening to public radio without contributing should seem wrong.)

Contract is a form of promise. A contract creates a kind of political order, a constitution, a specified range of reciprocal rights and obligations and contingent loyalties. You must not betray or deceive your partner. You must fulfill your obligations. You are free to leave an undesired relationship (you cannot agree to slavery, you are free to change your mind), but you may have to compensate your partner for the costs of the rupture. (Marriage, traditionally, was different. You could break the contract only for cause, some failure or betrayal on the part of your partner. Today no-fault divorce often poses fewer obligations on the exiting party than an employment contract or a lease.)

You can learn all this from an economics or a law textbook. It can be an inspiring vision of human relationship. Yet it also seems terribly formal. This is, I believe, an excellent model for the law of free relationships. But it tells us nothing useful about living in them. And what it does tell us, I believe, we will find misleading and twisted.

Again, the great problem with contract is that we cannot stop thinking about it in strictly economic terms. In our society in particular, to teach about relationships in this way inevitably suggests that our engagements with one another are a form of consumption. We select our vocation, our friends, our church, our mate from the options available in the great mall of society; we shop around, we pick what pleases us, what gives us "satisfaction." And if the relationship ceases to please us, we junk it and pick another. People, jobs, refrigerators, faiths, condos, laptops are all jumbled together in our minds. Do people actually live this way? You'd better believe it.

RELATIONSHIP, INQUIRY, AND LOVE

Obviously, we cannot stop with contract. We are going to have to say something more, something deeper, about the meaning of our individuality and our relationships with one another.

Contract is a perfectly general form for all human purposes. It presumes neither friendship nor love nor conformity to social customs and roles, but it can include any or all of these. It assumes that the parties to it will create the meaning of a relationship. All that it requires is that the relationship be freely chosen.

Sound familiar? That is what we were talking about as the essence of our search for one another. Each individual is unique, and thus each relationship is new. The true relationship emerges tentatively, gradually, hopefully, out of a mutual process of discovery that never quite knows where it is going and can never be quite complete. It is subject to joy, learning, communion, misery, frustration, and failure. People can grow apart as well as together. The true relationship is subject always to revision and reconstitution: hourly, daily, for a lifetime.

Like you, I am picturing friendship or love. But the image applies equally to all human encounters. Think now of a group on a camping trip. Think now of a committee in a boardroom. Think now of a seminar. Think now of a public meeting. Think now of all the readers and writers in the world. Churn these images around in your mind as you think about this. Are they not all about trying to find one another?

So more than contract, real relationship implies inquiry, just as it implies love as *agapé*. Inquiry in free relationships is self-constituting. It is unprefigured. It is corrigible all the way down and boundless. True relationship is about learning. Its end is transformation: of the individuals and the relationship. In inquiry we seek the uniqueness of the other, the others. But we are also probing for the wavelength on which we might reach the human universal, the wavelength on which we might get in touch with all our kind.

Is this is what we actually want to teach the young about autonomy? Conventional liberals teach autonomy so that people will be "free to choose." This seems to mean a sensitive awareness of one's own tastes and preferences and an optimizing rationality. Now, do we want to teach also that autonomy means having the confidence and the openness and the sensitivity to seek out the others, to try to understand them and thus ourselves? Do we want to teach them to start on the surfaces and probe deeper, through dialogue and inquiry, so that they may perhaps discover something at once intimate and universal?

CULTURE, RATIONAL PRACTICE, AND THE SOCIAL SELF

The idea of true relationship is enticing. But as I suggested earlier, we meet each other mostly through the rituals and routines, the "social constructs," in structured settings as we go about life in a world that is organized for us. We learn to work, love, and play softball according to the rules.

Custom and culture, manners and mores are important in our efforts to find one another, in our efforts to understand. We begin there in our quest to create real relationships. We may end there, acting out our roles conventionally, saying the expected things, if our efforts to find one another come to naught or if they lead to clash and contradiction. Among our own people, we are mainly with strangers. Politeness and manners, customs and conventional assumptions, no matter how banal and meaningless, no matter how trivial, can create a bond and even a caring among people where there may not be the slightest hint of intimacy.

The trick now is to pull the pieces together, to teach the young how to combine their individuality, their genuine effort to find one another, with the structured, conventional, rationalized relationships that give ordinary form and meaning to our lives. This is delicate work, and it takes good balance, but I think I can describe the essence of the process.

As individuals, we interpret and criticize practices. We learn to do them our own way. We look for improvements. We also do these things together. The band works for hours trying to define its own sound. We fool around together, trying to program the computer to do something very odd. We tinker with ideas, you and I (even as, in a certain sense, we actually are doing right now), trying to contrive a crushing response to the stupidities of current orthodoxy.

In such practical activity we become known to one another. We get to know each other in all our quirkiness through the ways in which we criticize, contrive, improvise, learn, founder, wander, wonder. We look for complementarities. We assess strengths and weaknesses, gifts and blind spots. We create roles, a division of labor and insight, a shifting situational sense of authority, of who should be in charge when. We find ourselves in these relationships. We live through them. We earn and give respect.

The experience is absolutely commonplace. We recognize it instantly. It is, for all of us, I believe, the source of much of our most intense experience. But this kind of relationship is not well described, either by the concept of contract or culture or, for that matter, by what we generally mean by work. It eludes the sharp dichotomy of the liberal "autonomous" self or the communitarian "socially constructed" self.

HUMANITY AND THE POWERS WITHIN

All I have added is the idea of inquiry and an ideal of true, primary relationship. I do this to deepen our understanding of contract and convention, not to displace them. And at the conclusion, with any luck at all, we may begin to see that the relationships that we want to forge with one another, the purposes that we seek, the enigmas and difficulties that we try to work out, are common to all humanity. They do not distinguish us, the rational Westerners, from people who live by other traditions, other codes. We are all trying to find one another, and distinguish ourselves from one another, through these four levels of our being, our individuality, our relationships, our culture, and our universal humanity. I think all four elements are essential to a full idea of what we should try to find in a free relationship.

The trick, I believe, is to keep these four visions of relationship in balance. I intend them as aids to navigation. You find your location, and set your course, not by following a single beam to the end but by triangulation.

Showing that relationships that are reduced to contract or custom are sterile and impersonal is easy enough. To come alive these relationships need the breath of people who are trying to know one another. But real relationships must be framed by the liberal ideal of mutual freedom, and they take their meaning from some vision of purpose and some structure of practice. And perhaps in the end any one of our kind would recognize the truth of such an assertion and say of course.

Surely, we do not intend to teach them to understand a marriage simply as a contract or a set of prescribed gender roles. A marriage is, to say the least, personal. It is created by two people trying to find one another. Nonetheless, the marriage takes life and form by the way the individuals interpret the expectations that they have learned about what a marriage is supposed to be and what it is supposed to do. And, of course, the parties must understand one another as free and equal: Each has chosen to try to create this union.

I believe that our thought inevitably has an Aristotelian, and thus universal, dimension. Despite all our liberal insistence that human relationships must be freely chosen, discovered, and fashioned by the parties to them, despite our conservative assurance that relationships do, and should, follow the lineaments of culture and tradition, I do not think that this is all we are prepared to say on the subject. I think we also need to say that some freely fashioned relationships are better and worse and that some traditions can lead people down the wrong paths in the relationships that they create.

I do not think that we are prepared to say that a family is anything that the parties to an agreement say it is or that all the rules that we have inherited define good families. I think that we believe that the family has an essential purpose, a human purpose, and that we can discern and deliberate that purpose in relationship to the amazing variety of actual family arrangements that people create and that cultures promote. By the same token, I do not think that we believe that a university or a school or a church is anything that freely contracting parties decide to call by that name, nor do I believe that our existing institutions, products of our particular history, embody all the qualities that such institutions should have.

Our power to question the practices and institutions of our culture and try to improve them comes, in the first instance, from the individual. But this power of practical reason is one we must exercise together in relationships. Amazingly, we can share these personal visions of essential purpose and work together to realize ideals that we sense we hold together in our minds. This takes place in our most intimate relationships, as in society at large. Is this not the most astonishing of human capacities? Is this not a power we should cultivate more self-consciously and together?

Negotiating the four levels of understanding is the heart of what we do in all our efforts to find one another, to sustain our commitments to one another. Minute by minute, day by day, for all our lives, we weigh these factors against one another in all our encounters. This is probably the most difficult work that we do. Finding the balance is hard. None of us is good at it all the time.

It should now be clear that we, the elders, are not doing well in this, our most necessary work, of teaching the next generation how to find one another and live well together when we say only, as so often we do, that they should do as they please or follow convention. This is very sad indeed, and we can see how the young are suffering from our confusion and our silence. Clearly, we have much more to teach, and we must begin to teach it. This is really a most urgent matter.

8

Teaching and Learning

We need the others for all kinds of reasons. We need them for affection, entertainment, security, production, and reproduction. But teaching and learning are intrinsic to all relationships. From the others we will come to know and to understand. Every time we gabble together, we teach and learn something: about Ford trucks, Wyoming, a good place to get oysters, inclusion, or the meaning of it all.

It is too bad that we tend to think of education specifically in relation to schooling. We know better of course. We know that we learn from every person we meet, every book we read. No matter how well the schools and universities framed our ability to understand, most of our knowing, our skill, and our meaning we found elsewhere.

So what we are talking about here is the whole astonishing process by which the human race picks itself up by the bootstraps and creates its own methods and its own awareness in each generation. In this total organic context we now ask: What do we want our legacy to be? We reflect again on our primary question: What shall we teach the next generation? But now we must ask the question not only of content but of pedagogy. We must ask not only *what* but *how* we shall teach the young.

The issue, as usual, is critical and practical. We are looking for improvement. The point is to examine our practices and make them better if we can.

The subject at hand is all the ways of instructing and illuminating that bind us together. I am concerned with the quality of the messages that we pass along in all the contexts in which we connect with and care for one another. This is indeed a fine theme for political and moral philosophy, and on the grandest scale. But it is also a down-to-earth meditation on how we can make the most of our individuality and our relationships.

Again, two images of the work of teaching and learning contend today in our public life. For the conservative the task for the elders is to pass on a legacy of language, history, custom, and skill, manners and morals, to make sure that members of the next generation grasp it, sustain it, and use it to frame the pattern of their lives.

For the liberal the aim is to create the conditions of personal autonomy. Liberals would teach the young to criticize, question, and to weigh. They would inspire in them a wary scrutiny of doctrines, stories, and received interpretations of the world.

I will try to negotiate the difference between these positions. To do so I must add two additional themes to the argument. First, the verb *to educate* comes from roots that mean to "draw forth" or "draw out" a power from within the individual, a power that is presumably common to all humanity. This is a classic sense of the aim of education, its source Platonic, from *The Meno*. Learning is like remembering something that was always there. And indeed in the language of cognitive structuring, we presume that the capacity for syntax, mathematics, and probably much, much more is prefigured in the physiology of the brain. Second, all teaching, and learning, is a direct and immediate relationship of inquiry, person to person. Here again are the four levels of understanding that we investigated in the last chapter.

One image focuses on culture, one on the individual, one on universal humanity, and one on real relationship. Each suggests a strikingly different idea of the educational mission of the elders and a distinct epistemology. But perhaps to find what we are looking for, we must accommodate all four. The task then becomes to define the most apt relationship among them.

CULTURAL TRANSMISSION AND INDIVIDUALITY

The conservative communitarian view is that teaching is primarily cultural transmission. Certain long-standing assumptions of the social sciences reinforce this idea. As the anthropologist Pascal Boyer points out, we really know little about how the process of cultural transmission works. In part, Boyer suggests, this is because of the way that we study such matters. Anthropology is interested only in cultural holisms, their transmission, diffusion, and survival over time. Anthropologists study "the Hopi way of life" or "Eskimo family relations." Furthermore, these social sciences implicitly accept a simple psychology of operant conditioning. People "learn" a culture, and that's the end of it.[1]

Boyer's interest is in cognitive structuring, the mind stuff that limits, for example, the kinds of religious ideas that a culture can create. Before we come to that, I want to take up the earlier question of how individuals react to what their culture has to teach.

As I say, those who think of education primarily as cultural transmission seem to believe that people simply learn a culture and accept it. And we know perfectly well that this is not the case. Individuals interpret and evaluate what they are taught. They accept, reject, modify, misunderstand, and create in relation to every single element of the lore that they receive.

The individual, then, in defining a life, in defining a self, selects from culture. And we have not the slightest idea of how this is done. We have no doctrine on the matter. Some of our choices may be chalked up to predilection or taste or accidents of character or temperament. Some may have to do with childhood conditioning. But some choices involve clear normative judgments. We think that this practice of our culture is wrong; we think that one is ennobling.

Consider the question of what the members of a church "believe." True, we can describe the doctrine of the Lutherans, the Presbyterians, and the Roman Catholics. Now look at a congregation of any denomination, and ask yourself: Do any two of these people believe precisely the same thing? True, you may find some dogmatic literalists among the communicants. But are any two dogmatic literalists literal in exactly the same way? Beyond that, most of the congregation has selectively affirmed this, denied that, and decided to reserve judgment on the other thing. Furthermore, some have understood some parts of the teaching correctly and missed the point of others. Would it not be fair to say that every member of the church has a different theology? Is it not true that this church, and every church, is only loosely, very loosely, tied together by a common set of beliefs? Is it not true that every religion is fundamentally a band of free thinkers?

I believe that it is always like that, that it is necessarily like that. Do you not find vivid individuals in the most homogeneous, traditional societies? It may be in order to speak of the Ojibwa or the Inuit, the Ibo or the Amish, way of life, but does not each Ojibwa, Inuit, Ibo, and Amish individual practice this way of life in a somewhat distinctive way?

We can, I suppose, imagine a perfectly compliant individual. Think of the most conventional people you know, those who do everything meekly, according to expectations. Do you actually suppose that these people have never decided anything fateful for themselves?

The process of individual response to cultural transmission is natural and automatic. Do those who think that the point of teaching is socialization want to suppress this process? It often seems so. In the name of shared affective relations conservatives often seem to seek a uniformity of understanding.

The point that I have made may seem a telling defense of liberal individuality. In fact, it is a cheap shot. The underlying issue is large and perplexing and leads to all the ambiguity of our public philosophy and its pedagogy. The student is inevitably going to interpret a teaching. But is not the task of the teacher to correct students when they miss the point or make a mistake? Should we not fail them when they persistently get it wrong?

In fact, the relationship between individuality and discipline in learning and teaching is intricate and subtle. We want to do things in our own way, to think for ourselves. Yet we also want desperately to learn. So we submit ourselves to instruction. We try to rid ourselves of our personal distinctiveness, and we try to think, act, and respond in the way that everyone should think, act, and respond. Thus do we learn language, arithmetic, every essential skill. Learning to do well in any field is an act of mortification, self-abasement, and self-chastisement. We try to extinguish individuality. Very much like a member of a religious order, we try to eliminate our own inclinations, our habits, and our will and to instill within ourselves, gladly, voluntarily, the habits of right understanding and the right way of doing things.

Perfection, in many practices, seems to imply the elimination of individuality. Again, in many rationalized techniques we essentially want interchangeability, that any skilled practitioner can be relied on to do the same work in the same way. We analyze a practice and program it to achieve the best reliable, repeatable results. Thus (up to a point) do we train pilots, cooks, police.

Of course, this is only part of the story. For learning also demands a personal engagement. We have to try out different ways of understanding and acting. We have to practice, ponder, experiment, turn things over in our minds this way and that, looking for the approach, the angle of vision, that works for us.

This tension between submission and assertion, mastery and creativity is inherent in all teaching and learning. It is one of the great dramas, played out often in our literature, our stories of ourselves. The delicate question for the teacher always is when to insist and when to let go. The delicate question for the learner always is when to submit and when to assert yourself, when to do things the way you personally think best.

It is important to understand that both acquiring a skill through discipline and defying the structures of established technique give us an enhanced sense of freedom.

The question, then, is how to resolve this tension well in all our teaching and learning. Let me propose a framework for understanding how this process might best move from discipline to individuality and back again.

THE UNFOLDING OF UNDERSTANDING

Instruction

Following directions to assemble lawn furniture, program a microwave, or get your e-mail requires neither understanding nor interpretation. You just do as you are told, blindly, dumbly, by rote. You know perfectly well that any creative intervention on your part will likely lead to disaster (which assumes that the instructions are correct and intelligible, two large assumptions these days).

The same is true of any task of memorization, as in learning the names of things, which is the first step in learning any sophisticated skill. We learn the names of the parts of the boat before we sail, the names of the organs of the body before practicing medicine.

Technique

At the next level individual response and judgment enter the picture. Consider first learning to drive. You have to be told the names of the parts and shown the basic operations. Then you have to try them yourself, correcting your mistakes, getting the feel for it. One marvel of our civilization is that most people can develop the motor skills required for what is, in truth, a fairly daunting task. And curiously, while you have to learn to do it yourself, the range of constructive interpretation is quite small. Driving is mainly a discipline. You learn to do it, mostly, just like everyone else.

Skills are arrayed on a long continuum, from those that require little in the way of individual differentiation to those that require personal interpretation to achieve mastery. In playing the piano, first you learn the names of the keys and to read music. Then you follow your teacher and play a simple tune. You learn more complex pieces. Eventually, you may try to imitate exemplars. But the aim of this all is that in the end you shall interpret, develop a style of your own, an excellence that is distinctively yours.

If you get this far, you may reach a major fork in the road. You may strive for mastery, to do a thing as well as it can be done according to the ideal (but historically contingent) standards of a genre or a school. Or you may break loose and become creative.

Note well: Creativity does not simply mean doing things differently. It means doing them better. Creativity is not any random act of self-expression. Creativity is always best guided (as is mastery) by that vague, elusive, but very real ideal of excellence or perfection or inherent purpose that lies mysteriously, beckoning more insistently the better we get, at the heart of the shared understanding of all those who have seriously taken up an art, craft, or calling.

Learning technique is a matter of submitting to discipline as the condition of being able to interpret, to express your individuality in the end. Would you be better off learning to write, swim, play the cello, use tools any which way, however you pleased?

Of course, we do not always seek perfection. One of the more important acts of our individuality is to settle for mediocrity, to decide to do some things not very well. Our culture teaches us to regard such decisions as failure, but they are in fact essential to any rational plan for life and nothing to be ashamed of. Given all the things there are to do in the world, given the particularity of our talents, deciding to be an indifferent tennis player or a slipshod gardener is an important act of personal autonomy.[2]

We will develop our own individual interpretations, even of basic skills that we all supposedly learn the same way. Teaching handwriting must be one of our society's most futile undertakings. Why do most of us choose this as a place to defy authority and give way to impulses of self-expression? We add our personal flourishes to the most routine, standardized activities: running a computer program, cooking an egg.

Technique, mastery, creativity, style, interpretation, settling for a level of incompetence, all these are acts of individuality that are inherent in the teaching of skill, best practice. As in all real relationships, the relationship between the teacher and learner, then, must be open, experimental—as in all inquiry, hypothetical. It is not always the case that the teacher wants more discipline, the learner more freedom. Frequently, the teacher is ready to send the learner out into deep water at just the point when the learner wants shelter and security. So teaching and learning, like any real relationship, is a matter of misunderstanding, making mistakes, apologizing, starting over, getting better at it. Teaching and learning as friendship, as something perhaps closing in on love, is an attractive ideal, however little realized in our own experience.

Interpretation

In any kind of relationship one of the most common forms of teaching is explaining, which is to say, telling others how a matter seems to us. This category covers an extremely broad gamut of our life activity. It includes much of our conversation, our professional statements, our writing. It ranges from gossip and shop talk to science and literature.

We tell stories. We reminisce. We describe. We diagnose. We write reviews and essays and novels. You tell me your views on global warming or Willa Cather. I tell you mine on the public philosophy.

When we instruct, people seek our fidelity to established knowledge. You ask me how many acres there are in a square mile. I say six hundred forty. I give you directions to city hall. I teach you how to sink a well. What others seek in such situations is not our personal impressions but our interchangeable and intersubjective knowledge. They want the truth.

However, when it comes to interpretation, our individual peculiarity matters. When our perspective is distinctive, it adds something to inquiry. We teach our own angle of vision to liven things up and to add depth and dimension to the subject at hand. We would learn little from a discussion of either death or taxes if everyone had the same views.

Note that interpretation is at the heart of real relationships. Part of friendship is instruction and the teaching of technique, but its essence is in exchanging particularity, which is how we reveal who we are.

Our interpretations are our own, but they do not come out of nowhere. Patterns of ideas that we have been taught suggest our interpretations to us, and those with whom we now inquire share these interpretations. Your distinctly odd ideas on divorce and remarriage are no more and no less than a particular take on the conventional wisdom of family relations abroad in our society today. Your thoughts on literature do honor to the schools of criticism in vogue when you were in school. Your reflections on your neighbor's personal finances reflect well on those who taught you to think in the language of rational economic calculation.

We are indeed cultural beings, but what is truly remarkable is the extraordinary variety of meanings that we can attach to what our culture intends to teach. Those who think of cultural transmission as passing on a body of custom and tradition that all will understand in the same way are bound to be frustrated.

However, there are crucially important issues here for those of us who would teach. For we do have to decide how far you can go in making knowledge personal before you have left the realm of the plausible, the permissible range of truth. This is particularly important for those of us who undertake to teach science, liberal democratic political theory, history, philosophy, all those schemes of reason that provide the framework for our common understanding. How far is each individual entitled to think about such matters in her own way, and how far are individuals bound, in reason and in truth, to abide by the dictates of the system? This turns out to be an extremely tricky business to decide, and most of the important philosophic quarrels of our age depend on how we decide it.

Disciplines of Inquiry

We tend to think that we start from facts and work up to theories. We gather a fact here, a fact there, and pretty soon, if we are lucky, things add up. We perceive pattern. Then we say we understand, that we have found meaning.

And we also think that facts are real and theories are conjecture. Facts have about them the quality of truth. But theories are interpretations; they are perspectives, they can be many. We could, if we wished, organize the facts in an entirely different way. Facts, we conclude, are primary and real. Understandings, we come to believe, are secondary and not to be trusted.

It works the other way around. Facts are derived from some discipline of inquiry. We notice things that fit a pattern of ideas we have learned. We also notice things that do not fit the pattern, things perplexing and unexplained, things we did not expect, anomalies. The former things reassure us and give us comfort. The later things puzzle us and lead us to inquire.

A curious feature of humans—especially, it would seem, of those moderns who believe that all is aimless randomness—is that we expect system. Our working presumption is that things are as they are for a reason. This enables us to recognize anomaly, and when we encounter anomaly, we have to suspect that either our observation or our understanding is wrong. Despite the weary skepticism, sometimes nihilism, that is so abundant in our time, we do persist in believing, a trait that seems inherent in our kind, that things should add up, some way, somehow. Thus do we expect our theories, our interpretations, to be true.

To talk together about just how true, or useful, or practical our theories and understandings are, we have to operate within what I shall call a discipline of inquiry. I do not want to give a too-tight definition of this concept. I am not, in fact, completely clear in my own mind on all that it might include. I am thinking mainly of things like scientific procedure and the protocols of specific disciplines—physics, geology—that are derived from it. Or I am thinking of liberal democratic theory and such derivative disciplines as law and political economy. I am thinking of Thomism. I am thinking of our grandest ideas of method. I am thinking of those great systems of fundamental propositions about the world and ourselves that we use to build our theories and understandings, to explain.

I think that we do know that our understanding is limited by what is possible within these systems. We seem to have a shrewd sense of just how much meaning we can expect to wring out of such a discipline. We know that a lot is bound to be left over. We have a special vocabulary to talk about these limits. We say that something is "nonsense" when it does not make sense within such a discipline of inquiry and we think it never will. Something is a "puzzle" when we assume that meaning exists that is compatible with such a system, though we have not found it yet. We speak of "mystery" when we think meaning exists but is probably beyond our grasp.

Teaching these disciplines of inquiry is a daunting task. First, students must grasp the pattern: They must see the forest, not the trees. They must not understand such disciplines as dogmas. They must recognize that these are not closed systems. They must see that they are designs for making inferences. As in Ludwig Wittgenstein's concept of a language game, they have to understand that they "point beyond themselves." Again with Wittgenstein, the object is that students reach the point where they can say, "Now I can go on from here."[3]

Now all these disciplines contain problematic assumptions, often big assumptions, about the world, about truth. Science assumes material reductionism. If you are going to practice science, you are going to have to think of the world as meaningless matter that you "explain" as the result of patterns that have no mindful cause. You are free to think otherwise about such matters, but in that case you are not doing science, at least not science as we conventionally understand it today. Liberalism assumes that all legitimate relationships should be based on self-constituting contracts. You do not have to assume that, but to the extent that you do not, you are not engaged in liberal political reasoning.

These disciplines are grandly ambiguous and pliable and porous at the edges. They discipline individual thought, but at the same time they open the door to interpretation and to art. Nonetheless, not all is permitted, and the teacher must make sure that students are clear about what is sense and what is nonsense in the particular scheme of thought, for such ideas structure our meanings of justice and truth. They are to be handled with great care.

The disciplines of inquiry must be among the most priceless treasures of our cultural legacy. And if truth were told, we do an absolutely terrible job of teaching them. Only the most minute fraction of the population knows how to use scientific procedure or liberal political theory or the logic of the law with creative familiarity and respectful precision. These are teachings that we reserve only for the most advanced professionals, for the "experts."

We assume that the rest of us can do without this knowledge. We do not even suspect that those who lack such understanding will be greatly impaired in their efforts to achieve personal autonomy, real freedom.

Most people are taught to see science or the law dumbly, as something beyond their ken—or worse, with fear, as something akin to a brute force of nature, not as a human enterprise. What is just as bad is that we teach the "experts" to take up just one such system, make it their own, commit themselves to it as adepts, and organize their entire view of life and the life process around it.

In the name of coherence and clarity we sometimes teach that living philosophically means reducing life to one mode of understanding. We should teach instead that such an effort will lead a person to live poorly. If you try to live by one system, your view of life will be constricted. You will misunderstand much; more you will not notice at all.

The best way to live is to have command of an array of such frameworks and to use them flexibly and experimentally, like a varied set of lenses, to take the measure of the world. Creativity begins when we superimpose a variety of schema on an object, to question, to see what happens.

To explain something we have to subsume it under some system of inquiry, some scheme of reason. Facing any ordinary outburst of human hostility, how do you try to understand it? Do you begin with a model of rational calculation and try to depict the situation as a set of strategies? Or is this a dominance game of some kind? Do you think now in sociobiological terms and ponder the behavior of the great apes? Is this perhaps a problem of political philosophy—are we facing issues of fundamental fairness? You consider St. Augustine: Is this a matter of the *libido dominandum*? Are we dealing with original sin? You review what you know about obsessive-compulsive disorders and the authoritarian personality. All the while, you proceed scientifically, experimentally, looking for the best fit between theory and data, the most adequate evidence.

The method is as old as judgment, a matter of trying diverse frameworks for subsuming particulars under general categories and principles. Note how different this is from the way that we train an expert to impose a privileged frame of reference on all situations. Note how this hypothetical, experimental way of proceeding is in fact more scientific than the expert's "rigor."

Note that this method of thinking does not subordinate the individual. You are not an instrument of the discipline, a mere technician carrying out its dicta. Rather, the disciplines are your tools, and the judgments of proportion, harmony, and propriety are your own, guided by that inner power that you also have cultivated to the point of familiarity, that power and that practice that make your rendering judgment appropriate and just.

The view is pluralistic. But this is not the pluralism of a multiculturism that insists that each individual must be embedded in a specific comprehensive system of understanding. This view supposes that the more diverse modes of inquiry that you control, the better off you will be. Nor is the view relativistic. The diverse systems of inquiry may reflect a partial reality, but it is a reality nonetheless.

People often say that they keep their science and their religion in separate compartments, for these are distinct areas of inquiry and reality. But it really does not work that way. Such schemes of reason complement and interact with one another. After all, I have been mingling science, political theory, classic philosophy, and theology throughout this inquiry. The truth is that all our schemes of reason, all our modes of understanding, connect in the end. After a while the distinctions between the scientific and the moral, the secular and the sacred, blur. Understood aright, prayer and inquiry begin to seem like the same thing. The processes of groping for God or for the meaning of the cosmos or for an understanding of another person are all extraordinarily similar—in the end, no doubt, the same process.

Dare we teach all this? (It would mean a radical change in many of our assumptions and habits.) Dare we teach also that our systems of inquiry are recognizably human constructions, that they point to but do not actually grasp a reality that is always elusive and that our intimations of this reality can guide our judgments as we use the disciplines of reason to try to understand? Our disciplines, our systems of inquiry, are approximations, but they are incredibly useful approximations. Perhaps one day we will do better. In the meantime the work is to learn to use them as instruments of our freedom, with discernment and imagination, mindful of their great strengths and of their limitations.

Universality

So as we now see, we have to understand the process of teaching and learning as taking place at four distinct levels. At the first level all teaching is a relationship between two people. At the second level all teaching must account for individuality, because we will choose to learn in our own way much of what we are taught. The third level is culture, the structured frameworks of thought, the disciplines, and the lore and stories of a people that contain most of what we teach and learn. The fourth level, then, includes the possibilities for understanding that we take to be common to all humankind.

What indeed do we intend to teach about this vast and uncertain potential? How do we plan to go about "drawing forth" the powers of the mind? And how do we want to go about understanding the relationship among these seemingly exclusive and contradictory levels of understanding? When do we want the young to see things distinctively, as individuals? When do we want them to see things our way, as our culture does? When do we want them to see things the way that, presumably, every person in the world can see them?

The ideal of common understanding is alluring. Is it not our most persistent, perhaps our most noble, hope that we might one day overcome differences, come truly to understand one another, and live in peace? This is the hope that we have to keep reasserting. It is perhaps the only way to keep our spirits up in the face of war, oppression, hatred, and all the barbarity, confusion, and missed opportunity that result from simple misunderstanding.

Obviously, we can understand things in very much the same way. We can comprehend one another. Astonishingly, humans are one species. Our minds were fashioned according to a common program. Neurophysiologically, we are set up to work in very much the same way. We have, as the ethical humanists remind us, very similar needs, aspirations, and capabilities. We are, the sociobiologists insist, commonly adapted both to caring and aggression. Platonists, and today cognitive scientists, remind us of the universal qualities of our understanding. Christians would show us how we all reflect the imprint of God. Liberals assert the ways in which we are equals, entitled to equivalent rights and respect.

Given our capacity for human understanding, what really requires explanation is the perversity of our constant misunderstandings and our frequent lack of interest in even trying to connect. Why is there at least as much hostility and suspicion as mutual comprehension among us? Let me first acknowledge the usual suspects: greed, ambition, fear, envy, and the like. But what I really want to explore is the uncertainty of our common understanding and how this emerges from the tensions between the individual, the cultural, and the universal levels of our thought.

The first problem with the universal level of human understanding is that it is indeterminate. We may all have the same capacity to learn a language, do geometry, sense injustice, experience beauty, and so on, but at the universal level these qualities are abstract and ethereal. To give them content we have to construct a determinate framework for understanding. Plato knew this. He did not just point to the forms. He constructed codes and curricula, as in *The Republic* and *The Laws*. By the same token, the indeterminate capacity for music within us is guided and expressed in forms and genres—the baroque, the romantic, folk, jazz. The construction is necessary, but so is the universality. Without the musical capacity there would be no music. The same is true of mathematics and language. A universal grammar may exist, as Noam Chomsky teaches, but this becomes determinate only with the construction of natural languages.[4]

The crucial distinction between the kind of classical idealism that I have been promoting and contemporary philosophic constructionism is that the classical idealist sees the construction and critique of constructed perspectives as always being guided by the universal human capabilities, whereas the pure constructionist thinks of them as free-standing, without foundations, and in need of no further explanation. The "cultural" level of understanding becomes all there is, and the "socially constructed self" becomes the essence of humanity. There is, oddly, no human universality. This is, in a nutshell, what the contemporary philosophic argument about truth and identity is all about.[5]

The great teachers must show us how to find the universal in the particular. Otherwise, we simply learn our language, our mathematics, and our law by rote, thoughtlessly. They must show us how our language exemplifies, but is not the essence of, language and how our law contains, but does not wholly capture, the meaning of justice. Only with this understanding can we become autonomous, live as we were meant to live, not merely as instruments of culture.

Somewhat mysteriously, this "drawing forth" of the inherent powers of our minds is something that we cannot do alone. This requires a midwife, a teacher. To make manifest our powers of language, we have to learn a particular language from others. We may have intimations of beauty and harmonious form, but they will remain brute and inchoate until we find a teacher. Our "awakening" to the universality of our powers, and thus to humanity, seems to require the assistance of another.

The purest, most enchanted, form of this relationship of discovery is the Socratic dialogue. The Socratic dialogue is a form of real relationship. It is a groping, probing effort to find understanding behind the hiddenness of distinct individualities, but it is also the effort to dig below this level to bedrock, to the foundation of understanding in common humanity, which is to say, in truth.

The Socratic dialogue is an effort to find the universality underlying particularities. It begins when the roles of teacher and learner are suddenly reversed. The one who before was giving instruction now questions. The one who previously was entitled to question now must respond. If both acknowledge the inadequacy of the teaching, the inquiry is free to proceed, as the search for meaning in all relationships does, hypothetically, critically, trying out options, abandoning trails, starting over.

Theoretically, the climax of the dialogue is mutual discovery, recognition of essential purpose, of the universality underlying the particular. But in truth the dialogue is never quite complete. Understanding is always tentative. Once more our finiteness, our individuality, intrudes. The universal can never be quite articulated or stipulated; it cannot be precisely put into words. We may think that we have reached common ground, but we can never be quite sure. The universal remains vague and indeterminate, as always. We continue to proceed by intimations. Our confirmation of common understanding is pragmatic. If we continue to agree that diverse particular cases do indeed fit under the common rule, we suspect that we are seeing the essential idea in the same way. If not, we must continue to probe. We can only know universals by the way that we appraise particulars. In effect, the quest to know the universal is an exercise in practical reason. Or better yet, every exercise in practical reason is a quest for the universal.

There is universal humanity. We know this perfectly well. All can feel pity for the lost child far away, across the continents. We can find the beauty in the tone of the Inca flute. But while there is human understanding, common humanity, the astonishing fact remains that, in our individuality, in our cultural distinctiveness, we will all understand it somewhat differently. Furthermore, for each of us there are realms of the universal that we do not understand. Each of us is blind to some facets of common humanity. Or we have not been "awakened" to them. These powers have not been "drawn forth" from our minds—if they are there at all.

Thus a realm of universal human understanding exists, and we all understand it differently. But why does any of this seem surprising? We have already seen that we will all think differently about the practices of our culture, the doctrines of our houses of worship, the teachings of our sciences. Do any of us use quite the same mental imagery to think about the Doppler effect, parody, the Renaissance, contrition, due process of law, synergy, malice, Platonic forms?

Our understanding of human universality arises from relationship, as all understanding does, with all the incompleteness, imperfection, and mystery of comprehension that relationship entails.

So we are left once more with the perplexity of our aloneness and our distinctiveness and the equal perplexity of our closeness and our comprehension—of those we love, our own people, and the rest of the world.

THE IMPORTANCE OF INDIFFERENCE

What saves us is our interest in one another. We are curious and we are concerned. Without this impulse, born both of our curiosity and our caring, we would be dumb and blind. At the same time we should not underestimate the value of the opposite human trait: indifference.

We are, again, distinct individuals. We are each of us warped, distorted, peculiar, specimens of universal humanity. We have our own temperament and tastes. For this reason we are largely indifferent to the interests and enthusiasms of much of the rest of humanity. We really do not want to enter into deep relationships with most people. We are delighted to stay on the surface. We skillfully contrive to avoid some people. That we engage in real inquiry with so few so seldom is further evidence of the imperfection of the world, of original sin, if you wish.

Our distinctiveness makes us charmingly perverse as teachers and learners. We are all convinced that the world would be better off if all could see things the way that we, personally, do. At the same time we scramble to avoid much of what the others wish earnestly to teach. Just as, in writing this, I am arguing that all people in the world should base their personal philosophy on things that I have found to be meaningful, so I will some day soon, I am sure, be warily and craftily trying to avoid an encounter with someone who insists that I should know the Lord the way he does.

Indifference is our great protection against overload, just as it is our protection against tyranny and oppression. When we come to feel as one with the leader or the crowd, our peril is the greatest. Perhaps it is time to celebrate, at least a bit, our aloneness and apartness, the fact that we really do not care to understand a lot of other people. Indifference is surely better than hostility and contempt, and hostility and contempt imply that we think that we have understood the other and that what we have found is appalling to us. To be sure, we can appreciate difference, be interested in the ways that others are not like us. But such appreciation implies distance, a sense that we are not going to come to share a great deal. In the end the sentimental ideal that we should all become as one, united with all the world in perfect harmony, would imply insufferable conformity.

We owe one another decency and respect. We are obliged to care for others, whether they are "our kind of people" or not. We need to be kind and civil. But we do not owe one another intimacy. That goes beyond our nature. And this is why we understand that universal love is an unrealizable ideal.

THE PRIORITY OF THE INDIVIDUAL

So how shall we teach the next generation? We know that we have a culture to transmit, an immense and impressive array of lore and technique that young people must make their own in their own diverse ways. We know that we want them to appreciate the many ways in which humanity is one kind, that we are indeed all brothers and sisters, though we know also that the universal dimension of humanity constantly eludes us, that we cannot in the end base an education, or a life, on this alone.

What we come to see, as we have suspected all along, is that the individual level of education is most important. The crucial part of passing on the legacy is one on one, dyadic. It is a product, ideally, of real relationship. Now the question becomes, inescapably, how do we intend to cultivate individuality in all the young who shall carry on after we are gone?

The first question that we must ask is this: *In what ways do we intend that every individual should be the same?*

The very ideas of education and cultural transmission imply that we are going to try to impose a contrived uniformity of some kind on that portion of humanity that is within our grasp. If our goal is truly to promote individual freedom, there are obvious ways, I believe, in which we should try to shape other people, try to make them come out the same.

Can we agree that we would want no one to be subservient? Is it not true that we want no one to feel unworthy of participation, as a full member, in the affairs of the world? Can we concur that we want no one to unconditionally surrender his will to another? To affirm such ideas seems unexceptionable, but we are perfectly aware that our affirmations are full of doubts and perplexities. Whether we want to use Aristotle's language or not, do we not suspect that some people are in effect "slaves by nature," that they would rather submit to the direction of others than determine the course of their lives for themselves? The crucial question is whether people should accept or resist this inclination. Liberals have never believed that freedom was necessarily a natural disposition. They have understood that people must be educated to it, that they must be taught to be free. By the lights of those of us committed to freedom, we should insist that others take charge of their lives to the fullest extent that they can.

Are we also able to agree that we want no one to be alienated, alone, cynical, isolated, without meaning? None of this implies that we must all be socially well adjusted. All kinds of ways of going it alone, of separateness, do not imply despair. The Desert Fathers never thought of themselves as alone. Most solitaries (writers?) indeed are not alone. They tend to live in deeper relationships with others, known and unknown, than most hyperactive extroverts.

And could we agree that we expect everyone to be responsible and skilled as parents, in their work, and as citizens? And could we also concur that although we may, as a community, want to enforce certain norms of good practice in these realms, we expect that each will carry out these responsibilities as individuals in their own way?

And this is to have said quite enough. We could go on and on, adding qualities and characteristics that seem essential to virtue and human flourishing, to the good life. We have a long impulse to create catalogues of virtue. The Roman Stoics in particular, and their descendants, from the "Mirror for Princes" writers of Persia to the popular proselytizers for virtue in our own day, have proceeded in this vein. They speak of benevolence, honesty, self-possession, generosity of spirit, tolerance, duty, and other good things. They speak of the understanding that inner tranquility is more important than the passing glories of the world. We could persist in adding categories, refining the qualities of good character. We begin to construct an image of the ideal individual, a single form for all humankind. The Stoic sage, the self-reliant liberal individualist, or the republican citizen may emerge as the ideal. But this is a graven image. Surely, we do not want to mold all humanity to one likeness. We admire too many individual possibilities to reduce them to one form. We do admire the virtues of the obstreperous, the single-minded, and the intentionally odd.

Now we see the danger of thinking of the public philosophy simply as something manufactured, a codified total doctrine that we forge in our deliberations. The more we try to reduce our philosophy to a bounded, articulated system, the more rigid and narrow we become, the more we exclude, the more contentious and unpersuasive we become, even to ourselves. We create a template for constructing the good person, and we recognize instantly that our stipulations are arbitrary. We create the ideal according to our dispositions, our taste and temperament. Or we create the ideal instrumentally: We look for human qualities consistent with the good functioning of a republic. But saying that is saying what?

For practical purposes this is why we are better off proceeding at the level of the essential, steering by our strong but elusive intimations of a reality behind appearances, our considered but still indeterminate sense of why human freedom and individual autonomy are important and how they might be fostered here and now, day by day.

We know that our powers to think at the level of the essential, of the ideal and the real, are frail and fallible. We know to be wary of our intuitions and the words that we find that initially seem to give our intuitions secure shape and substance. We know that we have to proceed warily, gropingly, feeling our way in the dark. This means that as we try to draw forth the individuality in those whom we are bidden to teach, we must proceed in dialogue and the search for real relationship, ready always to revise our teachings in the light of what we learn from the other in the encounter. No pedagogy, no practice, will enable us to overcome our lack of clarity and our own distinctiveness. We must teach in our own freedom, as the individuals that we are.

And again, we must remember that we, the elders, are in this together. We must advise and critique one another, encourage and admonish. We are parties to a common process, as necessary to humanity as it is mysterious. We are, after all, a teaching animal. We cannot, in morality, in instinctive nature, leave the young alone to grow up any which way. No one, not the most extreme relativist, can believe in total permissiveness. That is not even a human possibility.

"HANDS-OFF" AND "HANDS-ON" INDIVIDUALITY

Education must begin in the transmission of culture, technique, and skill, in the inculcation of good practice. We must persist in instilling discipline in the name of competence, responsibility, and solidarity. It is well if all face the same tasks at the outset, read the same texts, and meet the same standards in the name of equality.

Beyond this, in a liberal society the crucial task of education is the cultivation of individuality. This will occur spontaneously, of course, as individual perspective shows itself in interpretation, style, deviance, and creativity in relation to the elements of culture that we try to pass along. The next question then is clear: How do we develop individuality as an intention of our teaching?

I believe that two basic approaches exist for drawing forth the uniqueness of individuals and making this manifest. I call these the "hands-off" and the "hands-on" approaches to developing individuality. These are, at best, only loosely conjoined in our thinking. In fact, if truth were told, we have only the dimmest philosophy of how to promote true individuality. Perhaps this is something that we ought to think through. We might be able to do better.

The "hands-off" approach is implicit in the dynamics of open pluralist society. The idea is that throughout life the individual confronts a broad array of diverse opportunities and projects and is free to develop a personally satisfying pattern of engagements by choosing among them. The lifelong process of education, of the cultivation of individuality, is the exploration of diverse possibilities. Maturity, the discovery of the self, is the outcome of a continuous process of trial and error, success and frustration. We find ourselves, as they say, through experience of the world, by eventually matching our distinctive capabilities to the opportunities that we confront.

However, this "hands-off" conception of the promotion of individuality, however congruent with the presuppositions of liberalism, is never quite enough. We, the elders, must also draw forth the distinctive powers of each person hands on, one on one. We find each other in relationship with one other, through common projects. We come to understand ourselves in relation to the appraisals and the understandings of others, our colleagues in the common work.

And ultimately, if we are lucky, we will discover our uniqueness within common humanity through the explorations of true relationship with teacher, parent, supervisor, spiritual adviser, coach, friend. In trying to find one another, we must define our selves. We must articulate the strange effort that we must all make to understand the possibilities of our particular life in relationship to all other lives.

For the pure liberal, choice defines life. But the interpretation that we give to life, by our explanation of ourselves, also defines it. As the philosopher Stanley Cavell says, the moral life must be intelligible.[6] That is the point of Socratic inquiry, perhaps of all inquiry. In trying to interpret ourselves to another, we find ourselves.

The good society, then, is one that is open to a wide variety of individual explanations, one that has a broad vision of the possibilities of humanity. The good society, though, is neither passive nor lax. It will probe these explanations, question and challenge them. It will admonish the speakers to seek their distinctive best, to be skeptical of their interim answers. The bad society will try to conform one and all to narrow strictures. It will ridicule those who explain themselves subtly or with an edge. This is the only society that can actually be accused of trying to "normalize" humanity. It is not rare. Neither is it prevalent.

Do not imagine the good society as a kind of group therapy. Real relationship is, now and always, rare and deservedly so. We are simply lucky if we can find someone who can help us interpret our individuality. Thus the "hands-on" cultivation of individuality is not an item for the social agenda. It cannot be contrived as a matter of policy. But it is crucial that we, the elders, be aware that this deeply personal level of teaching is an imperative part of our task. Without it the legacy that we bestow on the next generation will be sterile and cold, capable of sustaining only meager life.

9

Community

We cannot make ourselves out of nothing. We depend on the elders to provide us with the wherewithal of life—food, protection, tools and skills, understanding. We should be grateful for these gifts. But what, precisely, does this gratitude commit us to? What is our duty to the community?

Some elders in every generation expect exact fidelity to the tradition. They expect us to perform the rituals exactly as we received them and with reverence and respect. The elders will look with favor upon the young who are dutiful. However, they will look with concern upon those who question or defy tradition. They may be, depending on the magnitude of their offenses, disdained or disinherited. These elders will shake their heads. They will lament the decadence of the present generation. They will predict the fall of civilization if things go on like this.

But this cannot conceivably be right. Blind obedience is not the duty of the young. Their task, their obligation, is to view their legacy with fresh eyes, to appraise it and restate it in light of the discernments of their reason, their best estimates of the justice, the excellence, and the fittedness of what they have been taught.

The elders have no right to expect exact faithfulness to their views. What they have taught is inevitably partial and groping. They have done their best. But the young now discern other possibilities within their legacy. Are the young being disloyal, unfaithful, if they pursue these possibilities?

To be sure, the young may not ridicule the teachings of the

133

elders, dismiss them cynically or in levity. When they recast and reconstruct what they have learned, they must act in dead seriousness. They may not rework their legacy just to be smart or just for their pleasure. They must understand that their necessary work of interpretation is the essence of their encumbrance, what truly binds them to past and future, to their community.

Some elders will not want the young to leave. They would bind them to their land. They will intimate that the duty of the young is to take over the firm or the farm, to be with them in their old age.

This is not right, either. Staying or leaving is not a moral matter. It is a choice, a decision about your vocation and your way, a matter of temperament and aspiration. Most parents, most elders, know this instinctively. There is a time to let go. The wise elders know that planning for this parting is a delicate business, a matter of giving the young roots and giving them wings, as some would say. But the parting is in our nature. The young must become independent, form families of their own, in their turn become elders. And some will go far away, for we are a species that wanders the earth.

We know that sadness lies in both leaving or staying. The choice is simply between lonesomeness and longing. All our lore and literature tells us that this is true. Those who leave will leave in tears, even as they feel a surge of freedom in their hearts. They will know homesickness and nostalgia. They will feel wistfulness for their home country, its smells, its sights, its ways, though these were the things they gladly renounced as they left. It has always been thus with emigrants. But those who stay will be wistful too, for what they do not quite know but for something missing, something unfound. Staying can also be a cause of estrangement.

Is the duty of the elders to teach the young how to leave? This would seem to be implicit in our nature. It would seem to be a tenet of our philosophy. Liberalism requires that all relationships be freely chosen and that all be reversible, for life is an uncertain voyage of discovery, and it is wrong to bind us to choices when we come to realize that they were mistaken. We have no right to

encumber the young by suggesting that they owe us lifelong defer-
ence and subservience simply because we bore them and nurtured
them.

Liberalism's historic enemy is tyranny, and we generally think of
tyranny as a public matter, the exercise of arbitrary and capricious
self-serving power by the state. But tyranny can be private too. Is
the role of government to protect the young against the arbitrary
and capricious self-serving power of the family or the school or the
church or the community?

Now we hesitate. We know we are entering treacherous and
murky waters. The question is not whether we shall intrude in the
affairs of the family. We already do. We protect spouses and the
young against abuse. Shall we protect them also against false
teachings, teachings that would render them servile, docile, unfree?

Shall we teach the children how to leave? Consider how U.S.
law treats the issue. In the case of *Yoder v. Wisconsin* (1972) members of the Old Order Amish refused to send their children to public schools and argued that they have a right to teach the young to
sustain the traditional Amish way of life, which abjures much of
the technology, skills, practices, and values of modern secular
American civilization.[1] But the State of Wisconsin argued, in turn,
that the Amish education fitted children only for an Amish way of
life. Was it not the state's responsibility to prepare all the young to
live successfully in the larger society? Was it not the duty of the
state to prepare the children, to give them the skills, to leave?

The U.S. Supreme Court ruled for the Amish on the ground of
freedom of religion but left the larger question hanging. Was the
effect of the ruling to submit the Amish young to the unchallenge-
able will of the Amish elders?

The dilemma here is one that we do not really understand or
debate. The issue is cultural pluralism. We think that liberal society should be a place where every group has a right to practice and
preserve its own culture. But what if these groups teach that
women should be absolutely submissive to men? What if they
teach that all should be absolutely obedient to the elders of the
tribe? What if these cultures smother their members in a teaching

that totally contradicts our commitment to individual freedom, to the proposition that no one should be taught to be subservient or in thrall?

As a matter of fact, the custom of our country is to sweep the young up at an amazingly tender age and carry them off to places where they are taught quite contrary to many ideas that parents and churches have tried to instill in them. Those of us who teach in universities take it as our sworn duty to bring the young to question many beliefs they picked up in the family, in the neighborhood, in the society. Are you uneasy about our teaching? Would you rather the elders got to inculcate the young exclusively in their own ways, their own doctrines of life? Or do we, officially, politically, as a people, have a duty to teach the young how to leave?

Shall we, then, teach the young that all relationships must be freely chosen and reversible? All relationships are experiments, conducted by hopeful but essentially innocent people, people reaching out for something they cannot quite identify, reaching toward something in the soul of another. Not all such experiments are apt to work out.

Still, does this bold, defiant, liberal doctrine actually capture the tone that we want? Should we not say something about respect and affection and gratitude to those who worry and fret about us and sacrifice and make us what we are? Such gratitude cannot bind us into servitude, but do we not have a duty to teach the young to understand that what they become depends on what they have received?

Finding the golden mean in such matters is difficult. "All relationships must be freely chosen and reversible." What, then, are we to say about marriage? To be sure, we are done with arranged marriage. But reversible? It should make us most uneasy, I think, to speak of marriage simply as an "experiment" that may or may not work out or a contract, like an employment contract, that we are free to quit when it no longer suits us.

I think that we do still believe that marriage is in essence a lifelong commitment, that this most amazing and demanding of human relationships implies unconditional acceptance, caring, and support. Do not the words of the Book of Common Prayer, "forsaking all others, to love and to cherish, for better or for worse, for richer or for poorer, in sickness and in health, until death do you part," still capture what it means for love to become steadfastness? Do we not still believe that these are the conditions of marriage, the excuses that we may not give for leaving?

And yet. And yet. People change, and no one is bound to cruelty or abuse. Should we not tell the young when leaving is right, if leave they must?

I think we must level with them. Marriage is the most difficult of human undertakings. We have no straightforward advice to give. In all its particularity, as we witness it in our lives and in the lives of others, the full meaning of marriage always eludes us. We cannot draw sharp simple rules about the obligations of the marriage relationship. Rather, we must come clean. We must tell them everything.

WHAT DO WE OWE THE COMMUNITY?

All relationships must be freely chosen. But to choose a relationship is to enter into the commitments that constitute a community. True, some relationships form spontaneously, without antecedents. Most, however, emerge when we join an ongoing project, a going concern. They are what lawyers call contracts of adhesion. You go to work or to college or to church. You join a profession. You move to a new city or a new country. You accept the conditions, and you take your place. You do not create a community. You join one.

Now, when you enter an ongoing community, you certainly do not expect to have things entirely your own way. You accept the terms, the operating rules. The very reason that you joined the enterprise is that you thought you would benefit by conforming to its norms and standards, by making its disciplines your own. Respect for the ways of the community is not simply a matter of courtesy or responsibility. It is your very point in signing up.

When we first join an ongoing association, we are like the young of the tribe all over again. We need instruction from the elders. We have to learn the skills and the practices. We have to find out how things are done here. We have to learn the difference between the sacred groves and the profane places and where to recycle the trash.

Most of this instruction is moral. We are taught the right and wrong way to do things, from the point of view of the elders, according to their philosophy. From the beginning, as is natural to all humanity, we have our own opinions about these teachings. But as novices, we are expected to keep them to ourselves.

Is the essence of our responsibility, our civic duty, being faithful to the practices and rituals of these communities that we have freely chosen? We are, after all, here of our own volition. We can leave at any time. We have, presumably, chosen this particular array of commitments in order to fashion a particular way of life. We have been welcomed in. We are, in a certain sense, guests.

This is, perhaps, a conservative view of our responsibility to the community. But, as we have already seen, this is not a full view of the process of learning, of the development of our powers. At some uncertain point we cross over. We cease being novices and become adepts. We have mastered the skills and can interpret the philosophy of the community. Now our responsibility changes. We have become citizens of the enterprise.

I do not think that we want to teach the young that they owe strict fidelity to the community, exact obedience and conformity to the rules. I do not think that is what respect or morality or civility or even common courtesy is all about.

As I said earlier, ritual fidelity is not in our power. We simply cannot do it. We are bound to interpret. In our individuality we will, willy-nilly, make judgments. In the firm, the profession, the city we will find some folkways, some prescriptions agreeable, some repugnant, and some just plain silly. We will keep our mouths shut about much of this, play along to get along. But we will make judgments; we will interpret.

Do we dare teach the young that what they owe the community is the transformative power of their own thought and sensitivity, their unique and distinctive ability to penetrate surfaces and get to the essences of things, the truth about things, the meanings of things?

What do we actually want them to revere and perpetuate? That they read all the same books or like the same music, that they remember the same dates or deeds probably is not urgent. What does matter is that they learn to penetrate to the heart of our teachings. Is it a great matter if they celebrate the holy days differently than we did? Is it not more important that they remember our musings about why something great and meaningful might be going on in the world? Does it matter if they remember the same battles that we do? Is it not more important that they grasp the significance of the proposition on which the nation was founded?

Precisely what they preserve of our way of life does not really matter. What does matter is that they come to see our ultimate meanings and purposes and that they keep looking for something closer to the heart of these meanings and purposes, something we cannot foretell at all.

Indeed, would we not want them to repudiate some of our ways and meanings—as in urban sprawl, the poisoning of the earth, our casual acceptance of radical income inequality that leaves women and children in poverty? Perhaps the only cultures and practices that deserve ritual fidelity are the truly sustainable ones, those that can be repeated almost endlessly without exhausting the earth. In many of its technologies and understandings our civilization is not like that. The young need not be taught to revere our improvidence or our indulgence or to be faithful to our poor husbandry and lax stewardship.

A total community, a smug community, a coherent community, a community that presumes to know all the answers and wants the young to be faithful to all its teachings, simply conceals reality. Such a community would put an end to mystery. However, a people whose elders make them aware of mystery, of how incredible and implausible it all is, is automatically an open society. A community that answers all the questions can only bring reverence to itself. A community that encloses all in certainty tries to protect itself against inquiry, which is to say, against yearning.

CIVIC VIRTUE AND PRACTICAL REASON

In classic liberal political philosophy, economics is natural but politics is contrived. We may truck and barter in the state of nature, but we come to the social contract gradually, self-consciously, in a certain frame of mind, one of "enlightened" self-interest. We see the advantage of reciprocity and mutual restraint and of government.

In the standard doctrine we are naturally calculators of pleasure and pain, of our personal good. But citizenship has to be learned; we have to learn how to think about the common good. How precisely shall we do this? What traits of character, what skills of thought shall we try to instill in the minds of the young so that they might in fact constitute a democracy? These questions are essential to what the political theorist Michael Sandel happily calls the "formative project" of the Republic.[2]

This work, we know, is necessary. We understand how fragile or how durable decent societies can be and how this fragility or durability seems to depend on a certain national character, certain moral traits widespread in the citizenry. To define civic virtue, and then to craft a civic culture, is serious business. It is something a free people must do well.

However, we also know that this work can lead to great foolishness. It may lead to simple indoctrination or pompous jingoism. Worse yet, it may lead to pious humbug, simplistic moralizing about the "virtues" of citizenship.

The trouble with most theories of civic virtue is that they suggest a single modal personality as their ideal. The good citizen is serious, deliberate, prudent, and public spirited. The good citizen argues and organizes, runs for office and debates the public weal. Such qualities and skills indeed are important. But most people do not like to do these things and are not very good at them. This image of ideal citizenship excludes most of us.

I would like to teach another idea of civic responsibility, one that makes the most of our individuality and thus of our need for one another, the necessary complementarity of our relationships. This would be an ideal of citizenship founded on our common, but highly differentiated, capacity for practical reason.

Practical reason, again, is an idea of virtue that comes down to us from Aristotle. It is the virtue of the judging, acting individual who, seeing through to the immaterial idea behind an undertaking, seeks an action that fits the need, or the work, of the moment. The political theorist James Bernard Murphy describes the nature of practical reason this way: "All skill is developed through the dialectic of conception and execution. By learning the general principles of a craft, the skilled worker is able to solve problems that arise in its execution, and by solving these particular problems in execution, he deepens his conceptual knowledge of the general principles."[3] The virtues of practical reason include creativity and caring, craftsmanship, painstakingness, and scrupulousness. This may be what love as *agapé* and reason amount to when they are brought together or seen as constituting the same thing. I believe this can be the core of a more complex and complete idea of citizenship than that taken simply from the requirements of liberal democratic or republican government.

The widespread exercise of practical reason leads to good practice, everyday excellence. Our ability to expect conscientious, reliable performance from one another makes the free life possible. Freedom, in our time, has little enough to do with self-reliance, strictly speaking. It has more to do with living in a dependable framework of interdependency, one that magnifies the individual powers of all, one that enables us to make remarkable plans with a high degree of confidence that they will be realized.

What we want from our airlines, our phone companies, our schools, our motel chains, our on-line services, and our police is that they will perform as expected when we call on them. The special temper of our age is to scrutinize all our technologies, all our procedures and methods, and perfect them if we can. We have tried to create reliable systems that perform with exacting precision time and time again. We have come to expect such perfection. We become sardonic, despondent, sometimes hostile, when these systems fail to deliver the miracles that we have come to expect from them, punctually, time and time again.

What is our responsibility to our community? The ethic of practical reason teaches both analytical creativity and meticulous trustworthiness. This ethic requires us to submit to a discipline in the interest of the freedom of all.

This ethic is, among other things, one of responsibility toward the treasures and beauties of Earth. The ideal of reliable performance implies sustainability. Any system that tends to self-exhaustion begs the question of what will replace it when it is gone. Perhaps the most urgent, and complicated, task for practical reason is to curb the wild gluttony of our age and to substitute for it technologies and practices that can endure. Such an ethic need not imply renunciation. But it does imply intelligence.

In many quarters the ethic of practical reason is not particularly popular. Some romantic individualists prefer to think of freedom only as self-reliance and self-sufficiency, but this often turns out to be a mean-spirited lonely ethic, for it assumes that the less that we call on others, and the less that they call on us, the better off we all will be. On the other side is the romantic communitarian belief that warm affective relations are always better than professional competence. Romantic communitarians prefer the caring neighbor to the emergency medical technician and think that the jolly bucket brigade has it all over the professional firefighters.

We provide the infrastructure of each other's freedom. Freedom in our age is a matter of precision engineering and absolute dependability. It also depends on an ethic of reciprocal trust and deep mutual honesty. These things exist. More than the cynic realizes, this is the working philosophy of our time and place. Alienated existentialists think that expressing their authentic anguish in the face of the absurdity of the world is heroic. The alienated existentialist fails to notice the heroism of the emergency room nurse, the schoolteacher, or the line crew after the storm.

The community of practice that is a profession, a craft, or a calling lives by a subtle ethic of practical reason, one that balances the requirements of disciplined responsibility with individual and communal critical inquiry in quest of a good.

In the first instance the practitioner, the citizen of a profession, is responsible for following the norms of good practice as currently understood. You practice medicine or teach calculus in the established manner. No one has a right to perform surgery or install electrical systems according to personal inspiration. First of all, the practitioner is responsible for best practice and reliable performance.

However, the professional is also a member of a community of inquiry. The professional has the right, and the duty, to scrutinize prevailing practice, to criticize it, and to search for a better way. But the professional cannot simply put a bright idea into action. You have to check it out with colleagues. The duty of the community of inquiry is to examine proposed innovations, test them and study them, and in the end to establish the standards of best practice. This is the rule, and the morality, not just of the sciences but of the crafts as well; it applies to carpentry, sheet metal work, and plumbing. This is our heritage of citizenship in the world of work, a legacy handed down directly from the medieval guilds.

Teach this ethic to the young, I believe, and you will teach them citizenship. Teaching them to vote, to deliberate, to be informed, and to attend to public affairs is important, but it is not the heart of the matter. The best communities, the cities and nations that stand out for their pride and their democratic vitality, are meticulous and caring all the way down. Things work right. The philosopher Eric Hoffer said that you can tell how civilized a nation is by looking at its maintenance records. A good community is one where the condition of the roads, sewers, parks, and playgrounds really matters. Bad communities are indifferent and rundown; things are scruffy and lusterless. Their citizens are callous and careless.

Good politics, I sincerely believe, follows from good practice. Teach scrupulousness in dairy farming, hotel management, and machine tool manufacture, and you will get scrupulousness in the provision of public services, the integrity of the courts, the quality of the schools, and the care of the air, the earth, and the water.

AN ETHIC OF INDIVIDUALITY

Communities are composed of the like-minded. We stand for things together. We are comfortable with the others. They think and talk like us. But this is not the whole truth. For the good community also values the individuality of its members, their sheer quirkiness and variety, for one thing but more than that for their ability to see and understand and do different things. Taken together, these qualities enable us all to see more, and understand more, and do more in common.

What we owe the community, then, is no more and no less than our particular vision and our particular talent. We have come out of the same past as the others. We have learned the language and the legends. We know the customs and the courtesies. But we see these things differently.

This is not something that we should keep to ourselves. We must not be intimidated by those who insist that we see things in one particular way, which is to say, their way. Of course, the unvarnished truth will be that sometimes we simply get it wrong. But this means that we simply have to change our minds. It does not mean that we should stop thinking differently. We have to go on seeing for ourselves and checking out our judgment against the perceptions of others.

Thus we also owe it to the community to think hard and seriously about the judgment of others. We are all teachers and learners here. Our duty is to praise and challenge, criticize and correct. Thinking that what others think is no business of ours is as wrong as saying that ours is the only way of thinking. We have a responsibility to treat all assertions as hypotheses and to examine the warrants and the evidence. Does this mean that I am again insisting on the rightfulness of the way of inquiry? Well, what do you say if the alternatives are rigid conformity to dogma or the floating relativism that insists that nothing matters, that you can think anything you please?

We have to appraise the performance of others. We have to evaluate the contribution of the others to the work at hand, for we have different talents and incapacities, and for each of us to serve where we are well fitted is important. To assess how a given individual can best contribute to the enterprise is always a judgment made in respect and love, for we all have special merits, and we all have distinct limitations, points on which we are awkward or things that we cannot comprehend. If such an appraisal leads to ridicule or contempt, it is wrong; that is a corruption of the proper function of evaluation. The great teaching is that measuring the contribution of others is better than measuring their worth or goodness or particularly their greatness. These things must not be confused. The person who has the ability to lead us out of the wilderness is not, for that quality, the better person. The person deft at keeping things neat and in good order may be the more valuable, if that is what we need at the time.

Not being considered useful in all situations is no disgrace. To be asked to play right field yet again is no humiliation. Things may be different when it comes to building the treehouse.

Evaluating others for their contribution is much more helpful than evaluating their morality. Too often, when we size up what we take to be the "character" of others, we display little more than righteous bigotry. To be sure, thieves, con artists, and shiftless free-loaders will dwell among us, and we must dispassionately and surely control them. But the ones we really have to watch are those who are eager to ridicule and condemn the weak and unfortunate and enthusiastic to chastise and punish them. These people, unfortunately, seem far more numerous than those who are truly shiftless and lazy, and they seem to be frequently in power.

We have to be the final judges in the case of madness. We have to decide whose minds are so driven by illusion that they cannot live successfully among us. Specialists can decide only the extreme cases. But in drawing the line between madness, oddness, and different insight, only we—ordinary people who also are touched by strangeness, fantasy, and illusion—can decide. Those who crave this work are in all probability quite mad themselves, and those who would very much like to avoid it are probably the only ones who should undertake it.

We must approach this work with great wariness, always bearing in mind that some of what at first seems madness is just the ordinary world seen from a fresh perspective. Consider the Book of Job. Consider quantum physics.

Let me sum up. To lay out this ethic of individuality in all its ordinariness tells us much about the images of community that we must not teach, the conceptions of civic virtue that we must warn against and condemn.

We must not teach that we owe the community literal, ritual conformity, that we must sustain the teachings of the elders exactly, with a reverence that implies compliance. We should warn against images of the virtuous life that reduce to one personality type and exclude many qualities of representative humanity. We must warn against those who teach that the rules were laid down long ago, that they are straightforward and clear and simply have to be followed. We must caution against the teachings of those who do not understand the muddled nature of our situation, of the deep ambiguities of the world.

We must not teach that the young must do the bidding of the managers or those who hold the purse strings, tempted though we may be by this hard-headed, tough ethic of defeat, helplessness, and resignation. We must warn them against thinking that the monetary rewards that they receive are a measure of their contribution. We must teach them the distinction between being the instrument of an enterprise and a citizen of the enterprise. We must teach those whom we think will become leaders to draw from within themselves the power to transcend cultural conventions and to see the governance of the institutions that they will lead fresh and clear, as a task of citizenship, as a social responsibility toward all who are affected by their decisions.

We must not teach the ethic of tribalism. We must not teach them that something deep and divine sets their people apart from all the rest. We must not teach that our duties, and our concerns, extend only to the members of our kind and that for all the rest, well, we are to stand aloof from them, uninterested and indifferent to their fate.

We must not teach that the community is no more than its government. And we must not teach that the community is no more than a construction of the powerful and that we must learn to stand apart from it, disdainful, however much terror and wistful loneliness such estrangement creates in our hearts.

For all its utter ordinariness, its unsurprising conventionality, this ethic of practical reason and individuality is contentious and inflammatory. Many will find these fighting words. But do we really intend to teach otherwise? In all seriousness do we not find the alternatives outrageous?

10

Working Relationships

The idea that we would be better off teaching an ideal of practical reason than raw, unadulterated Benthamite utilitarianism would seem to apply with particular force in the realm of economics. We are most confidently and sternly taught to think of ourselves as competitive interest maximizers, as economic theory drolly calls us. It is in our working and using lives, our lives as makers and growers, handlers and haulers, investors and buyers, that our aim, and it is made to seem a moral one, is to produce and serve so as to enhance the "consumer satisfaction" of others. If we do this well, we are told, we will receive a rich earthly reward, which we may then use to fulfill our own desires.

Society once believed that we should live frugally, reinvesting the gain from our productive and entrepreneurial labors so as to further multiply the prosperity of all. This was the teaching of the Calvinist entrepreneurs who created the Industrial Revolution in the north of England and in Scotland. Today such a view seems quaintly out of date. Now, it would seem, our goal should be simply dazzling accumulation, the pursuit of pleasure and power on the most monumental and magnificent scale. We are given to understand that those whose social product is the most entertaining, or those whose wealth comes from sheer speculation, will reap the greatest rewards. You cannot get rich, not really rich, simply by meeting human needs for food, fuel, transport, or housing.

Perhaps in simply seeking an intellectual position that was

148

neutral among competing notions of the good, orthodox economics adopted the pleasure principle. The result was a very strange, and very arguable, view of human motivation and human aspiration.

Contemporary market economics is starkly reductionistic. As we have seen, it portrays human reason simply as the calculation of gain and loss. It pictures all human relationships as relationships of exchange. (You can, and some economists do, portray the family as a system of exchange, of bargaining among parties each seeking to maximize their interests.[1]) The only ethic that such a philosophy can generate is an emotive and hedonistic one, and such a philosophy, of course, cannot take moral questions seriously at all. We do all this, as I have said before, in the name of skepticism, to avoid framing the problem of life around some particular conception of the human good. However, economics generates its own idea of human purpose. Aristotle thought this disgraceful. He wrote: "It would be absurd if . . . our lifelong efforts and sufferings aimed only at amusing ourselves. Serious work and toil aimed only at amusement appears stupid and excessively childish."[2]

Read any standard economist on consumption. Read John Maynard Keynes.[3] The aim is always "enjoyment" in some sense or other. In orthodox economics the motive for savings is "deferred gratification." It considers work a "disutility"—something unpleasant, something we seek to avoid. We work only to gain income so that we may satisfy ourselves through consumption. Those who work less than the norm are said to display a marginal preference for leisure. The language of orthodox economics insinuates a whole outlook on life that, to my mind, is misleading and demeaning.

In a longer, deeper tradition of economic philosophy, the aim of production is use. Is it not true that many of our exchanges are not consummatory but links in a chain, part of an ongoing, purposive human relationship? I do not buy a book simply to "enjoy" it. It is part of a collaborative relationship, part of the process of inquiry of my profession. Is this properly understood as consumption or investment? I know that economists are capable of talking of "intermediate" goods. But why do they insist that exchange must culminate in "satisfaction"? Why do they not stress that exchange is partly constitutive of relationships?

To be sure, the idea that the end of production is simply pleasure does apply to the seamier side of our economy. Much of what we produce is simply fad or fashion, pointless gizmo or pointless gabble, its aim nothing more than momentary diversion or that pitiable increase in self-esteem that some buy through conspicuous consumption. Many of our titans of marketing and advertising clearly operate under the impression that they are selling to Sodom and Gomorrah.

We tend to believe that the economics of the pleasure principle, the economics of the pure free market that has justified all the self-righteous giddiness of the recent past, is the dominant tradition of economic philosophy. This is not so. We have always seen the orthodox neoclassical position as contestable. In many quarters it is thought an aberration. Until quite recently, other schools of thought always challenged it, both academically and politically.

Many of these rival schools have their foundations, one way or another, in a deep, rich tradition of political economy that is rooted in the core values and assumptions of Western philosophy. I would like to recapture the image of our productive life that tradition contains. I believe it is much more compatible with the fuller liberal view of our humanity, of our individuality, and of the justification for our freedom.

THE GREATER TRADITION OF POLITICAL ECONOMY

The larger philosophic tradition of political economy has a long history. Its roots are in Aristotle. It was the normative basis of the medieval economy, both that of the manor and of the guild. Free-market liberalism contested the assumptions of this great tradition, root and branch, through the centuries. Yet, as we argued and constituted capitalist political economies, we retained or re-asserted many institutions and principles of the larger tradition, challenging the excesses, softening, humanizing the free-market system. This longer tradition has never been revived as a whole. Catholic political economy is based on it. So are the many variants of European corporatist thought, which run from fascism, through

Continental conservatism and Christian democracy to themes that run deep in European trade unionism and social democracy. Less frequently recognized is that the greater tradition strongly influenced American progressive and pragmatic thought and with it the closely related institutional-historical school of political economy.

In the long process of construction of liberal societies, free-market economics was never adopted and seldom argued in unalloyed form. It did not characterize American thought in the age of early nationalism, western settlement, or in the gilded age of rapid industrialization, and it was not representative of England in the Industrial Revolution or in the nineteenth-century age of reform. By the 1950s the general thinking throughout the industrialized West was that the free-market position was only of academic interest and an archaic interest at that. Capitalism was understood to be a planned and managed affair, thoroughly political, containing many elements from the longer tradition.[4] The emergence of free-market orthodoxy as a dominant position in the public debate after about 1980 astonished many of us. We did not see it coming.

The word *economics* comes from a Greek root that literally means "care of the household." The household, in Aristotelian thought, is one of a set of natural associations, including the family, the community, and the polity, that make our kind of life possible. The special concern of the household was with sustenance, providing for our material needs. Yet the task of the household manager was not simply production. The household was part of a web of relationships that gave life meaning and established just relationships among individuals.

The medieval guild reflected the ideal of the household. The responsibility of the master was to organize production, ensure best practice, train apprentices, and look after the welfare of all people associated with the guild. American progressive management theory of the early decades of the twentieth century had a distant but unmistakable echo of the household ideal. Progressivism taught that the leaders of the corporation were not responsible for profit alone but that they had a social responsibility to workers, customers, community, and the public interest.[5] Of course, the actual task of the manager of the Athenian household, as William James Booth, the political theorist, has brilliantly argued, was to organize the work of artisans, slaves, and women so that one man, the master, could be free.[6] Hannah Arendt seized on and magnified a theme in Aristotle, that the free life, the philosophic life, the public life, requires leisure, escape from toil.[7] And Marx, more influenced by Aristotle than is generally supposed, dreamed of a day when technology would make a life beyond necessity possible for all humanity.[8]

However, work that requires practical reason is essential to fully human life. As James Bernard Murphy explains: "What gives skilled work its dignity, according to Aristotle, is that a worker first constructs in thought what he then embodies in matter; conversely, what makes unskilled work sordid is that one executes the thought of another."[9] This need not lead us to lament the loss of pure craftsmanship, where a lone artisan conceives and executes a single piece of work. Aristotle, like Plato, Murphy emphasizes, taught a social division of labor that was based on ability and talent. This is different from the technical division of labor, which too often leads to the mind-numbing routines of traditional factory life.

Our work is a collaborative venture. The real work of management is to bring together unique individuals with their distinctive endowments in productive relationship. Our work, seen this way, is charged with all the significance of any human relationship. It becomes part of our quest for understanding of one another, our search for purpose. It involves teaching and learning. It entails responsibility for established practice and the critical quest for its improvement. It becomes a form of community. We are, ideally, citizens of an undertaking: We are part of a community of inquiry. Work is not a "disutility" in which we engage to gain the wherewithal to pursue "satisfaction." Nor should it be thought that the meaning of work as I have defined it is reserved for the few. Many, in our time and country, do find in work a vocation, an expression of their particular qualities and aspirations.

To visualize the management of the enterprise in Aristotelian terms casts a new light on the philosophy of entrepreneurship. Entrepreneurship, the creation and building of enterprise, is more than an act of financial acumen. We now identify enterprise primarily with the productive process and its constitutive human relationships. Outstanding entrepreneurs, I have long believed, are more apt to come from the engineering or operations side of the corporation than from marketing or finance.

To look at entrepreneurship in this way brings into question some current assumptions about business management. Today the business community often assumes that CEOs are interchangeable among industries. The CEO is simply a specialist in profit making. What is produced is of no particular importance. Wall Street views the corporation as just another fungible asset, to be bought, sold, traded, milked to secure higher earnings elsewhere, used for leverage or collateral. The CEO need not know much about the products of the firm or even take much interest in them. Thus we get editors who do not read and airline executives who have no love for aviation. The results are eventually apparent to one and all.

The idea of management as the just and efficient arrangement of individual capacities in productive effort has been the starting point for economic theory, the economist Joseph Schumpeter pointed out, from Plato and Aristotle through Adam Smith and beyond.[10] This and the idea of work as the transformation of thought into artifact are bases for the reconstruction of a political economy of practical reason. Such ideas are far more fundamental to the longer history of political economy as a philosophic calling than the hedonistic psychology and emotivist ethic taught by the currently fashionable "profit-maximization" and "consumer satisfaction" schools.

A political economy of practical reason needs a psychology different from that of orthodox economics. I have always liked Thorstein Veblen's thought that to found economics on "the pecuniary motive" was essentially arbitrary. You might do better, he wrote, starting from "the parental bent," "idle curiosity," and "the instinct for workmanship."[11] Veblen's list sounds offhand, but pondered carefully, it turns out to be a very apt statement of the human qualities fostered in this larger conception of political economy.

A political economy of practical reason leads to a more particular and situational ethic than formal economics. The ethics taught by contemporary economics is amazingly abstract and reductionistic. This reductionism, the "commodification" of everything, as Marxists used to say, was supposed to enable us to compare and evaluate very different things, apples and oranges, let us say, or Rubens and Rembrandt. Unfortunately, it does not work this way. Economics can ask, but it cannot answer the question of comparing utilities. We still must assign and calculate values, and that leaves us back where we started, puzzling over what we find more attractive or desirable or worthy and why.

Economic thinking is useful as a component of practical reason, but it plays a subordinate role. Once we have figured out what might be worth doing, proceeding as economically as possible is intelligent. Sometimes economic considerations can help us decide among options. But economic reason simply cannot teach us what is worth doing.

Again, the ethic of a political economy of practical reason is particular, down to earth, and situational. According to the economist Elizabeth Anderson, practical reason is inherently pluralistic.[12] There are diverse goods, and we must reflect on them differently, using appropriate measures of value and ideals of purpose. These may be subsumed under some overarching idea of the human good, but this thought is too lofty and general to help us much in comparing goods and making choices. Perhaps there are what the political theorist Michael Walzer calls "spheres of justice," but here the idea does not connote relativism or conventionalism.[13] What it implies is that those of us who are responsible for the production of a particular good must be immersed in its intrinsic worth and character. We must be cognizant of the tradition behind its construction. We must know and respect the ideals that have governed its creation and development.

THE ENTERPRISE AND PRACTICAL REASON

The method of practical reason, and the procedure of the community of inquiry, has everywhere a common metric. This mode of thought and understanding is universal, accessible to all people, like scientific reason, its close cousin. Yet its application to any practice or project is deeply particular. It takes an infinity of forms in what, precisely, it prescribes and proscribes for human conduct.

The best modern synonym for the Aristotelian *household* is probably *firm*. The term that I choose for a community of practice, in its economic aspect, is *enterprise*. By enterprise I mean the professions and trades, the arts and sciences, any productive association that is in principle self-governing. In business, then, the enterprise is not the individual company but the industry, a set of firms that share a technology, purpose, and productive culture, as when we speak of the auto industry, the banking industry, or the airline industry. The specific technological and normative order identifies the enterprise. Thus *agriculture* does not fully capture the sense of the term, but *dairying, citrus production,* or *wheat farming* might.

Each enterprise, in effect, constitutes a culture. At its heart is a conception of how things are properly done. Thus a morality, as well as a tradition and a way of life, goes with commercial fishing, book publishing, forest management, and the law. All this has an economic aspect, a concern that practitioners are able to make ends meet, but while that is a requirement, it is hardly the heart of the matter.

The enterprises constitute *communities* in the fullest sense of the term. They possess legacies that the elders pass on to the young, the new generations of practitioners. They invest life with significance for those who belong to them. They constitute a political loyalty that can be stronger than patriotism. Long ago the British political scientist Harold Laski observed that it was perfectly possible to be with your profession and against the state, with your church and against the state, with your trade union and against the state.[14] There are few enough causes for which I would go to the barricades, but academic freedom is one of them.

Such communities of work and calling, far more than most social commentators admit, have today displaced for many the historic solidarities of time and place, ethnicity and religion. Is this a good or a bad thing? Certainly, such solidarities, in all their specificity, fill in the details: They give concrete guidance in a society so complex that any overall philosophic counsel must be vague and indeterminate to the point of vapidity. To be sure, the communities of calling seem less organic than the communities of place and history that they replace. Fishing villages and university towns may weave together a total way of life from the practical ethic of their dominant professions. But such cases are unusual. Normally, the specialized philosophy of occupation fits awkwardly with other spheres of life. As I argued earlier, neither the norms of literary criticism nor those of police work suggest, on the face of it, a philosophy applicable to family relations or neighborly barbecues.

Indeed, such professional ethics may separate people and reinforce class distinctions. The professions that rest on higher education may create a culture that makes it hard for the practitioners to grasp the world as seen by those who make their living with their hands. The reverse, of course, is also true, which leaves lots of room for mutual misunderstanding.

The culture of a profession may become arrogant and insular, creating as much self-righteous isolation and bigotry as religion or nationalism. Haughty contempt among professions, as in the ritual disdain between business and academics, can lead to separateness and loathing that sometimes resembles ethnic intolerance.

Still, these ethics of a calling are a crucial, and a largely unacknowledged, part of our moral life and our understanding of the world. They give meaning and purpose, sharp and individual, to life. Often, when we think we are simply teaching skill, we are in fact passing on a philosophy, a system of value. We definitely should examine, more self-consciously, what we intend to teach in this manner.

To some extent the enterprise, the profession or craft, is rightfully autonomous. The community of practitioners is responsible for setting the standards, prescribing technique, seeking improvements.

Who else could do it? Yet the public has an interest in the performance of every enterprise. It is not the private affair of its community of inquiry, let alone its financiers. We depend on the enterprise
for the wherewithal of life. The question, then, is how this public
interest should be expressed. How should the public be incorpo-
rated into the political order of the enterprise? Through the years
we have discussed industrial democracy, public representation on
governing boards, pension fund socialism, and many, many other
enthusiasms for reforming the constitutional character of the
enterprise. Few have been adopted, and those that have do not
seem to have made a great deal of difference.

The orthodox economists assure us that an open society takes
care of all this. The market channels the process of practical reason within the enterprise, all this activity of criticism, inquiry, and
innovation, to the right result, the result that is in the public interest. Whatever the practitioners may think are the best products
and practices, the invisible hand guides their deliberations toward
the production of those goods and services that the people want,
in terms of serviceability, quality, and price.

In fact, the process is a good deal more complicated than that.
Within the enterprise some parties—engineers, physicians, artists,
professors, nutritionists, foresters—will hold out against the sov-
ereignty of the market. The protagonists of what is worthy and
what will sell will struggle in every firm, in every profession. The
issues of integrity, our own morality plays, are mainly of this kind.
Again, the orthodox economist reiterates the point: If the public
interest is the question, does not the market best resolve the issues?

In fact, this does not quite settle the matter. The difference
between competition among firms and competition among enterprises is great. In modern market society firms in an industry often
do not offer differentiated products. Rather, production has a
marked tendency to converge around certain dominant technologies, systems, and styles. Normally, a modest sort of price, service,
and product competition exists among firms in the same field, and
this does tend to keep the game honest. But at the same time this is
apt to be competition within a rigidly imitative conception of the
state of the art and assumptions about what consumers desire.

Competition among enterprises, between rail and air, coal and oil, Internet and mail, orthodox medicine and alternative, is something else again. Here the market truly does reflect competition among different products and practices, technologies and industrial cultures. This is also the competition of the "creative destruction" of technological change, as Schumpeter calls it.[15]

Progressive political economic doctrine taught that the state had a role in managing the enterprise so that it served the public interest. While the community of inquiry of the enterprise might be the source of standards, the state had the responsibility to underwrite the regulations of the enterprise, to make them enforceable and general for the industry. This was thought essential to protect the quality conscious from the unscrupulous, who would compromise quality to cut costs.

Progressive political economy also held that the services of certain enterprises—power, transport, communication—had become so essential to human well-being that the public had a responsibility to ensure reliable performance and universal access. Thus government constituted such enterprises as public utilities, regulated monopolies, charged them with providing a service to all citizens, and guaranteed their profitability in exchange for their forswearing the opportunity to deal preferentially with the most profitable customers.

The progressives thought that the public ought to debate the performance of particular enterprises, that citizens were entitled to be part of the community that governed banking, oil, the railroads, the stockyards. Today, despite public contempt for the shabby performance of the airlines and the medical insurance companies, the pure free-market economist wants to shame us into accepting what they provide. Our complaints are elitist. You just want the airlines to be the way they were when only a few were able to fly. Until recently it was thought unseemly to question the practices, indeed the motives, of for-profit health maintenance organizations: Don't you know there is no such thing as a free lunch?

Again, impartiality is the first commitment of skeptical liberalism. The state should not give preference to any way of life or idea of the good. Thus in the utilitarian political economy the state should only be concerned with the aggregate performance of the economy, the sum of satisfactions available to individuals. The state is concerned with things in general, nothing in particular. Its place is not to decide what goods to produce or what services people require. It follows that it is out of place for citizens to debate and deliberate such matters, as though they were public issues.

The vision of the economy represented to the public thus becomes increasingly ethereal and abstract. We are to evaluate the economy only in terms of specified indicators of success. The task of the economy is to produce growth and wealth and jobs with price stability and balanced trade. Precisely what is produced is of no moment. To ask whether we have too many shopping malls and not enough open space, to inquire into the deterioration of the manners and morals of the television industry, to consider the impropriety of clear-cutting native cedar is considered vaguely indiscreet. The market will take care of all that. The strictures have been again stated by all the champions of the pure free market, and we are duly chastened. Really, we have no cause to complain. The goal is "consumer satisfaction," and we have only ourselves to blame.

EQUALITY, ELITISM, AND THE MARKET

The raw Benthamite version of utilitarianism is starkly egalitarian. All pleasures and pains, all individual calculations of better and worse, are to count the same. To quarrel with the quality of the social product is arrogant, elitist. To urge policies that would induce the media to produce more intelligence and taste, less banality and sleaze, is simply presumptuous, an effort to impose your tastes on others or, worse, to coerce others into paying to support them, as in public subsidies for wilderness recreation, public radio, or the arts. High-mindedness is a matter of personal preference. Poetry is no better than pushpin. Classical music, professional wrestling, pornography, sylvan glades, and scuzzy bars are all equally elevating or offensive. It is all a matter of taste.

The case for the market seems impeccably democratic. We feel justly rebuked when someone raises it in response to our complaints about the quality of our culture. Even John Stuart Mill, who really wanted to, could not find a satisfactory answer to it. In fact, however, the case for the democracy of the market is suspect, in some ways fraudulent. The market is not responsive to individual preferences but to money, and nothing in liberal philosophy suggests that the preferences of the rich are to count more than those of the poor. It is perfectly obvious that a society like ours produces more yachts and luxury resorts and less affordable housing than would one with a more equitable distribution of income and wealth. The case for capitalism has a contradiction that cannot be resolved. The case for income inequality, on the production side, simply does not square with the case for the equality of preferences on the consumption side.

However, the story has a great deal more to it. A free-market economy will indeed promote excellence if its entrepreneurs and inventors, its engineers, writers, and scientists fix their minds on the problem of practical reason rather than that of consumer satisfaction. The point is not new. It has long been part of the standard apologetics for a free society. We have just neglected it in the giddiness of our times.

Consumer demand does not much drive those who engage in practical reason. Anomaly, limitation, the intimation of something new motivates them. To be sure, the engineer, seeking the soul of a new machine, hopes it will be salable, just as the writer hopes for readers. But unless the writers or engineers are hacks, they are not much concerned about "satisfying" demand. In fact, in the process of critique and innovation that is the heart of practical reason, they could not, even if they wanted to, be guided by the goal of "consumer satisfaction," for at this stage of the game the consumer does not know what to demand.

Those who engage in practical reason, then, the true entrepreneurs and innovators, have a different nature than those who follow the crowd. Their object is not to give the people what they want but what they think they should have. The true entrepreneurs have always believed that people would think themselves better off with electricity, cars, telephones, railroads, and personal computers. But they did not ask them. They did not take surveys.

The mentality of the creators is not by nature one of responding to demand. Rather, they are pursuing in thought something that, when produced, they hope will be prove worthy and useful. The advertisers, of all people, have always understood this. They know that they must teach people what to want. Capitalism does not respond to demand; it contrives it.

This is certainly not to say that everything that is created, everything that finds a market, enhances the overall excellence of the civilization. Many artifacts of our commercial culture are simply clutter. We have the weird complexities of creative finance, the rococo of software, the baroque of retailing. None of this is significant. Every art and science has its decadent side.

The essential point is that if a free society is to pursue excellence, those who engage in practical reason must be dominant over those who calculate the bottom line. Those who are motivated by "the instinct for workmanship" must prevail over those motivated by the "pecuniary instinct."

It is not that the mass market demands sleaze. Rather, sleaze is a function of the culture of an industry. Those who produce tasteless, exploitative work for a hypothetical lewd, vulgar, mawkish, thirteen-year-old male mind-set have not actually inquired deeply into the potential preferences of their audience. What is more likely is that the producers of such trash have lewd, vulgar, mawkish, thirteen-year-old male mind-sets. Mass taste need not be ugly. Democracy is probably not the problem. Ordinary people have always responded to some things that are fine and some things that are not. Junk will always have a niche, just as the superb does. The trick is to expand the range of normal excellence, to make the commonplace quite good enough. John Stuart Mill knew that.

The consumer is still sovereign. What will be produced, its incidence and distribution, is still a function of the market. But we cannot attribute the quality of our artifacts to the taste of the people, and a sorry defense of shoddy performance in any industry is to say, "We're just giving the people what they want." The quality of the goods and services that we receive lies in the moral sense of each industry. Walk down the aisles of any store. Consider the high quality of our domestic appliances and our tools. Explain the mindless design of so many of our electrical fixtures and lamps. Then answer me this: Why are women's clothes shoddy and men's well-made, systematically, across the industry? And why does no one discuss this?

WORK AND VOCATION

The orthodox economists are simply wrong about us. Nor do they have a moral worth teaching. On the whole we do not, nor should we, spend our days in the calculation of gain. The point of life cannot be to relentlessly accumulate assets so that you can retire young and avoid the "disutility" of work. There is no honor, neither is there glory, in negotiating the biggest "compensation package" of them all. Something is seriously amiss about a school of thought that would represent humanity to itself in this way. I do not believe that very many people put the ruthless pursuit of gain at the center of their life plan, nor do I think that many people view those who do with envy. Most of us, I believe, think of them as warped personalities. Most of us, I believe, think that they are as much to be pitied as censured.

Some people are, indeed, authentically interested in the intellectual gyrations of finance. It is an absorbing game. Profit is the object, perhaps, but the pursuit of it as an art form is probably not greed. (Motives are always mixed, of course, and who can distinguish the lust for power, or for acclaim, from the lust for art in the writer or the scientist, let alone in the speculative trader?) To be absorbed in finance in this way is indeed a vocation and no different from being absorbed in mechanical or literary matters. Finance is a necessary human undertaking, part of the infrastructure, like roads and sewers. It supports our work, but it should not define it. When that occurs, we lose all hope of integrity. I believe that we have a duty to make all this clear in our teaching, in the legacy that we hand down to the next generation.

Ideally, work should be a vocation. It should be an outlet for that "rational love" that is as close as I can come to defining *agapé*. It should be an expression of our distinctive abilities. It should be an exercise in complementarity, thus in inquiry and discovery, a Buberian "meeting" with other individuals. Work should be part of our quest for understanding. It is part of our search for a place of our own in the world. It is also a means of earning a living. Of course.

Many find just such satisfactions in work. But we must also teach that work does not always approximate this ideal, and for many it never does. Work is, by its nature, repetitive. The cataract surgeon, the philosophy lecturer, the ferry boat captain, the cook, as much as the factory worker, do the same task, the same way, over and over again. The fascination pales. Days stretch out, monotonously the same. The surgeon takes special notice of a change in the tuna salad in the hospital cafeteria. The cook complains of a change on the label on a can. Our worlds narrow, settle down.

To work is to be of service, which means putting up with others of our kind. If you take their shekel, you do their bidding. Work often takes us into a theater of the absurd, full of strange discordant expectations and disharmonies. All bosses, all clients, must be presumed, simply as an operating rule, to be mad. Office talk is frivolous and boring. Talk on the job site is arrogant and self-serving. We put up with one another. Barely.

Our work frustrates us. At the end of the day things have not worked out at all the way we wanted. We are at it again. We are measuring the world, and our efforts in it, against an ideal that exists only in our minds, and we are trying to make the world conform to that ideal. We are only being human. This, in the most humdrum manner, is our divine discontent.

Good work, in this sense, is, I believe, the ethic of most people. We are not, most of us, meant to be economic maximizers. Rather, we try to realize the vision within us. We reel against economizing constraints, often to the point of the quixotic. The doctor can barely hide her contempt for the business manager of the HMO, the engineer his for the penny-pinching of his client. And this is just the point. Is not "the instinct for workmanship" stronger than "the pecuniary motive" in most people? Should we not teach that Veblen had it just about right?

Our teaching of all this need not be stern and didactic. We simply have to reassure the young that their instincts are right. We just have to lay to rest the idea that we are other than what we are, that we are not, as some do teach, calculating machines.

INDIVIDUALITY AND JUSTICE

As the political theorist Thomas Spragens has wisely written, any contemplation of the irreducible differences between individuals should provoke in us a sense of tragedy and a stern understanding of fate.[16] Our attributes as individuals are gratuitous. We simply *are* male or female, tall or short, black or white, smart or dumb. Some of us have Down's syndrome, and some of us do not. Some of us are born on the back streets of Calcutta, and some of us are not. If you think about these fateful differences carefully, I would think, you might be led into a blind fury against a creation so random, so chaotic and callous, in the distribution of attributes among people. No story can be told about this, no fable can be created, that makes any sense of it or makes it all come out all right. Considering these facts, one at a time, in detailed particularity, should lead you right into thinking that the world is meaningless, a grotesque joke.

It may also be, as Spragens suggests, that contemplating this tragedy opens the problem of justice to us. We do discriminate among people. We do not treat all alike. We think it proper to treat people differently, according to their worth, their contribution, their needs, the legitimacy of their dependencies, the evil they commit. When we consciously consider our conventions of discrimination among people, we engage in constructing a theory of justice.

The orthodox economist assures us that in a free-market system the problem of justice will take care of itself. We all produce to meet the wants and needs of others. Those others pay us what they think our product is worth. Those who produce what others value deserve a rich reward. If millions will pay a few dollars to watch a champion athlete perform, that person deserves income and acclaim way beyond the common lot. If no one will buy your hand-dipped candles at the art fair, you do not deserve a dime.

The case is just good enough to be enticing. It does account for those entrepreneurs who, through hard work, persistence, ingenuity, and organizational skill, have indeed made our lives better. But our long-standing myth of the "self-made" person who "built this business all by myself" deserves scrutiny. All by yourself? Without an education, we suppose, or financial backers, advisers, suppliers, workers, agents? *All* work is collaborative, and distinguishing the value of the contribution of any specific party to it is difficult. Which, again, is why even the exceptional reward of the heroic entrepreneur requires examination.

And, again, how much of the distribution of wealth and income in this society can be explained as neatly as the orthodox economists would have it? Wealth begets wealth and status, status. Luck and contacts enter in. How much of the disparity of wealth and income that we see about us is deserved? How much of it is necessary?

Some people think that sharp income differentials are necessary to encourage superior performance, perhaps to induce performance at all. The premise, again, is that work is a disutility that people will avoid unless driven to it by carrots or sticks. The assumption is that under conditions of relative income equality, no one might ever lift a plow again. I do believe that just compensation for superior performance within any occupation is a problem. And I believe that we have a major problem with our assumptions about just differentials between occupations. And I do not believe that the market can settle many of these problems.

Many grounds can justify differences in reward. We may talk of differences of responsibility, effort, risk, deferred gratification, need, and the like. Few, considered carefully, provide much of a defense for the status quo. Inquire thoughtfully into any of these dimensions, and you will find deep and disturbing questions about what we have conventionally been led to believe.

Consider responsibility: How do we justify our standing assumption that those who supervise have greater responsibility than those who actually do the work? Do principals have more responsibility than teachers? Do CEOs have more weighty responsibilities than engineers? Is the responsibility of the physician less than the business manager of the clinic or HMO?

Consider risk: Is the risk of the miner, the commercial fisher, or the police officer less than that of the investor or start-up franchisee? Who taught us to think that only capital risk counts in these calculations?

Consider effort: Does the brain worker necessarily work harder than the physical worker? Does the manager necessarily exert more effort than the employee?

Consider deferred gratification: The medical doctor spends, let us say, ten years in education outside the workforce. Thus the doctor has foregone, let us say, ten years of income at $25,000 a year to become a doctor, or $250,000 in all, and, let us assume, another $200,000 in educational expenses. Let us say that the doctor practices for thirty years. Should we then pay doctors $40,000 a year?

Consider need, in the case of the legitimately dependent. For those seriously handicapped, those legitimately exonerated from responsibility for their own support, we pay a subsistence benefit. Why should we not pay at least an average income, because these people have been deprived of the opportunity to earn such an income through no fault of their own?

All the standard justifications for unequal reward have a moral, a righteous, tone about them. One deserves more than another for undertaking more demanding tasks, forsaking leisure, exercising greater care and diligence, perfecting skills, and so on. The unmistakable insinuation is that all people can rise to the top if they would just get up and exert themselves. Hard work will be rewarded. But most people will not put forth the effort. They are, at heart, slackers. They prefer their ease to the disutility of work. But we, the industrious, deserve to be well-off. The rest deserve no better than they get. They should count themselves lucky that we, the hard working, have made jobs for them. Are we not all familiar with such self-righteous humbug?

None of this speaks to the matter of justice with which we began, to the quite obvious unfairness of the distribution of initial endowments among individuals. This is the issue that we really must address. Now we must decide, as a matter of politics and policy, whether we want to fight against the unfairness of the world, the manifest injustice of creation. Do we care to take up such a vain and obviously futile effort?

John Rawls suggests that we deserve no credit for the use of talents that we got quite by accident.[17] Why should we give exceptional reward to those who simply can manipulate abstractions, negotiate compacts, excel at basketball? Some say that we must give incentives to those who possess rare talent to induce them to develop their skills. Does it not seem to you that to possess a rare and useful talent, like intelligence, and to refuse to use it unless you are given exceptional reward smacks of blackmail?

Rawls argues that the only legitimate reason for differences of reward is that such differences work to the advantage of the least well-off.[18] But Rawls has few enough followers. He created no movement. This is not an issue that, for the moment, the prosperous want raised. The well-to-do, quite obviously, want silence on this matter. The less fortunate today seem to feel little overt fury. They blame themselves. They accept inequality, their lot, as a matter of fate, a fact of nature, the way things are.

How, then, do we intend to represent this matter in what we teach the next generation? What shall we say about all the accidental differences between individuals, differences that seal our fates, that determine whether we will be honored or disdained, what meaning and significance our lives will have, to ourselves and to others?

These gratuitous differences separate us. Great gaps exist in our capacities to know one another, across sexes, across circumstances of birth, across differences of talent and perception. I shall never know what playing music magnificently is like. I shall never know what being humbly simple, trustingly obedient is like.

Yet these great, strange, random differences that separate us are also the sources of our commonality, of all relationship. When we discover our own one-sidedness, we recognize our need for the others to complete our being. This understanding of complementarity between opposites, which fate has decreed should be our lot, may be divine, as in love, or prosaic, as in work.

The essence of the division of labor, of all our working relationships, is to understand that our differences are the basis of our need for one another. To understand one another deeply and fully, in all our possibilities and incapacities, and to harmonize these capacities to create something fine and useful is what "care of the household," or entrepreneurship, is all about. The rest, the "truck and barter" of Adam Smith, is just filling in the details.

The mutual respect of those who rely on one another in a work of difficulty or precision cuts through all the prejudices and stereotypes of surface society and takes us into a more earnest world. The trawler captain has absolute authority but depends, absolutely, on the skills of the crew. What looks like hierarchy is in fact strong equality, equality beyond any preconceptions of superiority or inferiority, dominance or subservience, equality defined morally and psychologically as mutual respect. In the moments when this actually occurs, life probably is about as good as it gets. This is close to the core of the meaning of our humanity. This is why work, pure and simple humdrum work, is so important.

In understanding this, we play a part in defying fate, that fate that has recklessly tossed us out, broadcast, in such a strange array, cast us forth to land any way we may, without explanation. Only when we see that this absurd diversity is not meaningless, dumb, pointless but that it can be fashioned into a pattern of purposeful cooperation, do we, I believe, do what political economy was intended to do, and it then becomes the grandest of studies.

We do not think this way very well these days and that, I believe, is a peril. Part of the reason that we do not see the possibilities of our complementarities clearly, I believe, is that we have come to isolate ourselves by type from one another. The manipulators and the makers, the planners and the producers, live in isolated communities. They do not mingle, so they do not see the possibilities in one another. This was not so when all the skills were so much more visibly coordinated with one another, in the small shop, in the farming town. Now we do not actually meet one another. We encounter one another in stylized transactions. We are abstractions to one another. I do not believe that this is a good sign.

More than politics or love or church or community, work can lead us to a deeper appreciation of one another, in all our difference, in all our strangeness, and can lead us to recognize the full humanity of one another, as we understand our dependence on one another, and our need for one another.

Does all this bear on the politics of merit and reward, on the problem of justice, in a free-market society? You bet it does. We must take this question up again as soon as we can see through our current hypocrisies, as soon as the weather changes.

11

Democracy

Democracy is the political form of free relationship. It is part of the process by which solitary individuals, all of one kind yet each utterly distinct, try to find one another. It is part of our search for personal identity and common meaning. It is an aspect of our effort to coordinate, to overcome our mutual incompleteness.

Democracy is a necessary part of a free society, as are contract and the market. Yet the visions of democracy are many, and they rub uncomfortably against one another in our collective mind. Democracy can describe a utopia or a prosaic way of running a government. I believe that we must pass along both the ideal and the matter-of-fact versions of democracy. The young will need both if they are to govern themselves well.

Pure democracy is a peculiar ideal and epistemologically interesting. The basic thought is that a free people can create its own culture, its own philosophy, and its common sense of the meaning and purpose of life simply by talking it all out together. In effect, we pull ourselves up by our collective bootstraps.

Thus Hannah Arendt imaginatively described a mythical Athens in which free individuals deliberated the good life and the good society and then created its rules, its roles, its moral code, the character of the state. As in a theater, each played a part, and each was in part the author of the drama. The Athenians played to one another. They were their own audience. They appreciated the distinctive interpretations each brought to the role he played. They won honor and recognition, or shame, as they played out the scene that they had created.[1]

The problem, of course, is that this ideal of democracy as a self-constituting order requires people who are already awake and aware. Only they could create a polity in which all could live philosophically. This is very different from the problem of creating democracy among people who are often in awe of leaders, docile, conformist, grasping, pedantic, prone to obsession and fantasy, as well as at times wise, empathetic, patriotic, and aware of their finitude and fallibility. In other words, the problem of ideal democracy is how it could arise among people like us.

Pure democracy appeals to that contemporary academic insistence on value noncognitivism and relativism, to a politics that can be shown to be without foundations, without antecedent philosophy, floating, held up by nothing more than sheer consensus. And, indeed, more than enough of the philosophically inclined today teach that truth and justice, rightfulness and beauty are just what a particular people at a particular time think they are.

Pure democracy looks perfectly neutral. The self-constituting people needs no prescriptive tradition, no elders, sages, or great lawgivers. Rather, the people themselves decide the life worth living and create a government to give effect to their decisions.

But does this not imply that the people could will anything and call it right or wrong, true or false, just or unjust? The will of the foundationless, absolutely self-constituting democracy has no provision for appeal. But do we not also know that absolute majority rule can be just another form of tyranny? And does it not seem that precisely when a people is surest of its convictions that individual freedom—and truth—are most in peril?

In fact, pure self-constituting democracy is not at all relativistic. The antecedent conditions, the foundation principles that a people must accept if they are to call themselves democratic in this way, are very stringent, and they lead us back to a very specific ideal of the human good and the life worth living that is, for us, by now extremely familiar.

A pure democracy must endorse the principle of equal citizenship. Obviously, it will not do for the people to decide that the will of the most active, the most revered, the richest, or the most numerous should prevail. You cannot stack the deck and claim neutrality.

A pure self-constituting democracy must absolutely guarantee equal citizenship. But what does this imply? To be sure, all must have the rights of freedom of expression and association, the right to vote and to hold office. But this is hardly enough. If democracy is to be constituted as a true community of inquiry, all citizens must be presumed equally competent to deliberate the meaning of the common life and the aims of law. As the German philosopher Jürgen Habermas has argued, all citizens must be able to put forward conceptions of the common good and argue them and to weigh and criticize the view of others. No one should feel psychologically subordinate, inadequate, or encumbered by prescriptive tradition or convention.[2] We are back where we started from, with a society of the already philosophical.

Pure self-constituting democracy is, then, hardly foundationless. Rather, it is built upon a very specific, and a very utopian, human ideal. What is more, such pure democracy requires, as philosophic presupposition, a commitment to the rule that all public decisions are provisional and subject to revision. The moment that a community of inquiry decides that it has reached irrevocable truth, it ceases to be a community of inquiry, and it ceases to be a democracy. It becomes a closed community, a community of dogmatism or tribalism or fanaticism. The first rule of inquiry is that we can never finish the search for truth. The first rule of democracy is that there can never be a last election. These are the same rule.

The effort to reduce democracy to pure procedure in the interest of impartiality leaves us perplexed. The conditions of such ideal democracy are so severe that they could be realized, if at all, only fleetingly and in very small groups. Still, we could proceed in another way. We can say that the role of democracy is to interpret a prescriptive tradition or a public philosophy.

This is an instrumental view of democracy. The object now is not, as in pure democracy, to constitute a people ex nihilo. Rather, the object is that a new generation reflect on its legacy, the teachings of its elders, and decide how to construe them in its own time. The point seems Burkean, and indeed it is. Perhaps democracy in this sense could pertain to the interpretation of any tradition. But in our case, of course, the tradition in question is quite explicitly that of liberalism, of individual freedom.

LIBERAL DEMOCRACY

John Locke, as later Thomas Jefferson, assumed that all people could see the "self-evidence" of certain individual rights and that the object of government was to secure these rights for the people. But they did not believe that the implications of these rights, or their application to particular cases, were simply transparent. Rights had to be interpreted. The task of a government of representatives of the people was to transform these abstract principles into an impersonal and publicly known body of law. Quite conventionally, I call this understanding of democracy "liberal democracy."

In such a democracy the common good is not whatever the people will. Nor is the object of political deliberation taken to be the construction of a public philosophy, an ideal of the public good. That is taken as given, by an act of initial commitment. Now the task of deliberation is to determine how to secure, sustain, and perfect a regime of individual rights.

Liberalism is not an axiomatic system from which we can automatically deduce right answers. It is more like an open matrix for thought. Liberal political theory provides parameters for choice, but it does not tell us how to reconcile its strong categoric principles. It poses puzzles and paradoxes for judgment.

We know these dilemmas by heart. They are the common currency of our politics. We believe in freedom of expression, for we cannot imagine why those who are dogmatically certain should be permitted to silence the rest. But does this mean that we must simply acquiesce to a culture saturated with crassness and lewdness? We believe in equal opportunity. But what does equal opportunity require? Is it enough to legislate against discrimination, or do all need equivalent educational foundations, rights of occupational and residential mobility, perhaps relatively equivalent income? When is a person legitimately excused from the duty of self-support?

When should a person be entitled to an income from the state? Where is the line, in the whole tangle of unlike cases, between the sphere of individual free action and intrusion into the private domain of another? What is to count as a harm? Is noise a harm? Are demeaning remarks?

What is the source of this capacity for political judgment that we expect of the liberal democratic citizen? Is it natural or is it learned? Every Enlightenment philosophy supposed that liberal democracy rested on universal capacities of ordinary reason. Cultural determinists would believe that the discernments of liberal democratic reason are a tradition like any other and must be learned. But in fact we know nothing about the human capacity that makes liberal democracy possible. It seems a strange and uncertain power. In some—extreme libertarians, gun lovers, the politically correct—it can degenerate into fanaticism and dogma. It can grow feeble and fail in the most statesmanlike. It can be affirmed, defiantly and with subtle skill, by ordinary people under duress, as in the civil rights struggles.

Except in law schools, we make little effort to cultivate this capacity for political judgment. Only a very few university graduates take courses in political or moral reasoning. What passes for civic education today is a patchwork of bits of history and constitutional knowledge, some fragments of political science positivism or realism. The idea that politics is a skill, and should be taught like any other performing art, would be met in most quarters with incomprehension if not derision. It is a wonder that the Republic still stands.

Perhaps the capacity for political judgment is a talent like any other, one of those universal human capacities that is unevenly distributed among individuals and can be warped or thwarted, cultivated or ignored. If this is so, not all citizens are likely to display the same competence in political deliberation. To say this should not lead us to embrace the charming old notion of a "natural aristocracy," a representative democracy in which ordinary citizens identify their "betters," who then go on to deliberate and decide the public good. The incidence of the capacity for political judgment is uncertain. It can turn up in just about anybody at any time.

In a liberal democracy the needed insights generally come from unexpected quarters.

All liberal democratic theory presupposes that we are naturally partisan. We are partial and our perspective is limited. In justice, we feel, we should receive what the others receive. We perceive no distinction in the cases. Others, of course, see the matter differently. But the issue is not just self-interest. All talents are personal and imperfect. Those with a gift for music do not see the meaning in the score in just the same way. Doing science is a very personal matter, in a way a matter of taste. Why should not the same be true of the gifts by which we discern justice?

From the beginning liberal democratic political theory has taught that our need for government is at base a need for an impartial arbiter. And in the end only we, the rest of the citizens, the momentarily disengaged, with our varied abilities to seek justice within the ambiguities of liberal democratic theory, can do this.

THE CONSTRUCTION OF LIBERAL
DEMOCRATIC SOCIETIES

A strange belief, the product of the very way that our public philosophy was originally written, is that liberal democracy is natural, that it will emerge spontaneously whenever the hand of oppressive government is removed. Such a view was unusually prevalent in the last decades of the twentieth century, no doubt because of the exaggerated enthusiasm for free-market capitalism in that time. Thus, when the Soviet Union fell, the expectation was that capitalism, and democratic government, would simply emerge, vibrant and triumphant, from the ashes. That, of course, is not what happened.

The fact of the matter, as the economist Karl Polanyi taught long ago, is that the free society is a planned society.[3] It is the product of massive intentional state action. The culture of individualism and the market generally comes about through a conscious revolutionary transformation. It is by no means natural, what will happen inevitably if government stays out of the way.

The road to the free market and the free society needs careful preparation. The people must create a common law and replace old patterns of privilege, hierarchy, and monopoly with an integrated comprehensive system of open contractual relationships. They must develop a common currency, a banking system, all the institutions that provide the infrastructure for free commerce and the free life. They must provide public education, policing, sanitation, and transportation. This was the pattern of development, first in Britain, then across Europe, in the nineteenth century, and even then the path to liberal democracy on the Continent was halting and uncertain.

In the United States the kind of comprehensive planning that the free society requires is most strikingly evident in the design for development of the western lands. The square survey, the careful provision for the use of the land for education and internal improvements, are part of a comprehensive philosophic vision of how the investment of public capital in a continent would lead to a particular favored way of life, a smallholder democracy.

The process of constructing a liberal democracy is unending. Liberalism, again, is not a closed intellectual system like, say, arithmetic, which gives specific singular answers to every question put to it. Rather, liberalism is an open system of inquiry; it requires interpretation.

The heart of liberal democratic politics, then, is that the people decide what kind of liberal democracy they want to pursue in the next period. This is what partisan politics should be all about. The aim is to control government and advance a program that will draw liberalism toward one of the emphases inherent within it, which basically means correcting course, in the direction of either liberty or equality.

The politics of liberal democracy is a philosophical politics. But it is not an absolutely self-constituting politics, a pure deliberation on the good life without preconceptions, as the ideal democrats would have it. It is rather a working out of the details, and a working through the riddles, of a public philosophy that is the foundation of the common good.

This process of interpreting and deciding the proximate course of liberal democracy is deliberative, but it cannot be the intimate deliberations pictured by the participatory democrats, the democracy of the ideal town meeting. This must generally be democracy at the level of the nation, of mass politics, a politics of coalition and mobilization. Indeed, the politics of slogans and advertising is degenerate deliberation. But under the best of circumstances the role of the ordinary citizen can be little more than affiliation and voting. This always seems a primitive way of deciding which nuance of liberal democratic politics we should now pursue, but at this point our capabilities for further deliberation are usually, for the most part, exhausted. We have gone about as far as we can go with collaborative inquiry. All we can do now is let the people decide.

The decision to construe liberal democracy this way or that will necessarily advantage some and disadvantage others, and democratic politics will become a politics of interest. What might once have been a politics of inquiry is now transparently a politics of rhetoric, of shrewd lawyering, the cynical packaging of ideas obviously distorted, for they show no attention to the ideas obviously at issue, no effort to seek out approximations of the truth.

What is more, the work of the continuing construction of the liberal democratic regime necessarily takes place in an environment where democracy is imperfectly realized. Even if all are citizens, not all are equally citizens. Democracy thus always entails a struggle for power. Inherent in the idea of democracy is that the project should be completed, that all should become equal citizens. Also inherent in this project is that the effort to achieve completeness will seem threatening to those presently advantaged. And in liberal democratic logic the only argument possible for sustaining an incomplete democracy is that any effort to enhance equal citizenship must pose a threat to present liberties.

At this point the citizen who believes in democratic inquiry becomes frustrated and disillusioned. But this is precisely the point at which liberal democratic inquiry must go on. Now it is crucial that the process maintain its integrity. For liberal justice still requires that we decide when people are entitled to be treated equally and when they are entitled to be treated differently, At the moment of our greatest cynicism and disgust, we must be at our most discerning, for however deceptive their rhetoric, those who have an interest in some advantage may also have a right to it. And those whom the liberal democratic project must now in justice favor may have said nothing at all.

A WARINESS OF GOVERNMENT

What indeed do we intend to teach about the role of government in a free society? Americans have passed on, generation after generation, a surly, malicious contempt for public officials, a cynicism about politics and a mistrust of the state that most Europeans think verges on paranoia and often achieves it.

In part, of course, this culture of contempt for government is a partisan affair. Those who are advantaged by the incompleteness of democracy are the ones who teach it. "Big government" is the necessary instrument of political inclusion, of equal citizenship.

Some say that the characteristic American hostility toward government is a positive cultural trait, that it is a reason that we have preserved our freedom. Let down our vigilance, become compliant, and we will soon be submissive victims of an Orwellian bureaucracy that is just waiting for us to let down our guard. Then it will pounce.

I know that some people believe exactly this, but it is strange doctrine. The free life requires respect for authority, support for competent, energetic government. Fortunately, every generation has had a defiant minority that has dismissed the rhetoric of contempt and taught that public service is a high calling and politics a worthy vocation. Thus we have always had a saving remnant that has ignored the rancor and skillfully gone about the people's business.

But scrupulous government requires more than an outstanding public service. The task of citizens must be to scrutinize the work of government, criticize, urge, and demand improvement. And the fashionable contempt for government is just another form of passivity. We can, after all, do nothing. All politicians are corrupt, all bureaucrats inept and idle. Why get involved? That will only encourage them. Let us just sit back and complain some more.

We have grown indifferent to the whole problem of citizenship. Our popular attitudes lead to detachment from the public realm. We have turned the electoral process over to consultants and manipulators who are so bad at what they do that instead of enticing people to support the cause that pays them, they have managed to disgust the citizens, to turn them off from the process almost completely.

We are playing with fire. It is time that we consider the legacy of liberal democracy that we intend to pass on.

THE DEMOCRATIC RELATIONSHIP

Like all our relationships, democratic relationships are incomplete and uncertain. We may seek solidarity in democratic politics, but in the end conflict, misunderstanding, and mistrust remain. Democracy is not a way out of our separateness. It does not solve the mystery of our individual identity. In the end we are still alone.

Liberal democracy does not try to overcome this separateness. Rather, it opposes all those forms of politics that produce contrived solidarity, a simulacrum of the mystical union that we crave, the political kingdom. Liberal democracy understands that some arts of politics can produce mass euphoria or hysteria, committed subservience, or rage at the outsiders. For those committed to liberal democracy, the greatest evil is the effort to end our longing through politics.

Liberal democracy assumes that we cannot overcome our separateness; it is part of the human condition. In this liberal democracy simply echoes the wisdom of our philosophy and our religion. It partakes of the view that the essence of our nature is to recognize our imperfection and our incompleteness and that we long to overcome this imperfection and incompleteness. We take liberal democracy to belong to the secular realm, but its teaching is precisely the same as our faith. And liberal democracy is not at all relativistic or skeptical about this. Its teachings are quite definite on things first and final.

Liberal democracy provides the same check on solipsism, on our internal certainties, that other communities of inquiry do. It requires that we check our judgment with the others, that we justify ourselves to them as they must justify themselves to us. In this sense liberal democracy simply assumes, as does our philosophy and our science, that we are engaged in a quest for truth.

Scientific procedure and liberal democracy represent different but parallel methods in our search for understanding. Scientific procedure stands for the brighter, more optimistic hope, the possibility that through painstaking investigation, checking and rechecking, we might just come to see some things in the same way.

Liberal democracy represents the darker, more realistic thought that difference and discord will always remain. It does not assume that we will converge on a single point of view. Soberly, it counsels how people who are fated to see the world quite differently may achieve a life in common.

These two great methods of human understanding must be taught together. The young must see that they are complementary and intertwined. If you teach only that you should assent to nothing but that which has won concurrence at the end of the most rigorous critical inquiry, as science does, you forgo all the possibilities for mutual tolerance, compromise, and getting on with the work at hand that liberal democracy entails. Teach only that concurrence is mainly a matter of accommodation and aggregation of rival standpoints, as liberal democracy does, and you foreclose the possibility that we might have good reason to come to a common understanding of the nature of things, as science teaches that we can.

But neither of these great methods is simply a technique of conflict resolution. For liberal democracy, just as science, insists that we scrutinize our efforts at common understanding, seeking always to perfect them, to bring them closer to an order that we find latent in the world or in our hearts.

What we learn, then, is that politics is one form of our relationship with others, but it is by no means the fullest or the final form. Democratic relationships are ideally congruent with all other relationships in a free society, those of friendship, love, learning, community, and work. They are relationships of discovery, of an effort at understanding among distinct individuals. They aim at common purpose, and they aim at excellence.

Politics may be the means to our self-construction, but it is important to teach that we must construct ourselves in truth. We can imagine virtually no fantasy that we might not persuade ourselves to play out in the political realm. We can come to believe that we are the slaves of the Sun God. We can imagine ourselves fighting for the true faith against heretics and transgressors. We can tell ourselves that our prosperity is a sign of our righteousness and thus our right to rule in every realm.

Liberal democracy insists that we must not found ourselves on our illusions. Rather, we must begin with our finitude and ignorance, the mystery of our identity and our destiny, and find out what we can by working the question through together, with all the means at our disposal. This does not mean there are no democratic illusions. They abound. Liberal democracy is no guarantee against fantasy or profound error. But it is all that we have. And its aim is truth and not illusion, which is not the case with most other forms of politics.

PART IV

Humanity

12

Who Do We Think We Are?

STORIES

What do we intend to tell the young about humanity, about the fact that we are all of one kind, obviously the same and yet obviously different from everything else in nature? What shall we say about where we came from and where we are going and about the astonishingly odd fact that we are here at all?

Perhaps, you say, we should tell them stories as we always have. We tell stories to children to reassure them and to put them off until they are ready for the truth. But what, then, do we intend to say when they are ready for the truth and can be put off no more?

Well, you say, we make up more stories, just as every civilization does. Every people has a creation myth, a story of where the world came from, and a foundation myth, how our people began and why we live the way we do. All civilizations exist on myth and fable, legend and story, and for all our stern talk of science and reason, we are no different, or so they say.

But what kind of stories shall we make up now, now that we are self-conscious and philosophical, now that we are quite aware that we are children no longer, now that we know perfectly well that we are making up stories to cover our frightening ignorance? We can no longer pretend to innocence. Now we know, and this is the great success of the philosophy of self-consciousness and of critical theory in all its forms, that our stories of reality and who we are are our own compositions. We make them up. And that implies that we now, seemingly for the first time, have some choice in the matter. It appears that we can decide what kind of a story we are trying to tell. That means that we have to make some estimate of how things actually are.

How shall we go about doing this? We are, after all, strangers in a dimly lit land and strangers to ourselves. Is it not appropriate, then, to start with our ignorance and our awareness of our ignorance? All our philosophy, and all our religion, up to now, has started with the strange, unfathomable sense that we have of a gap between our understanding and the way things truly are. Is this not the right place to begin? Is this not the most striking peculiarity that all of us, people of all cultures and creeds, all humanity, have in common?

We have at least this much to work with. We know the immediate neighborhood. We are, as I have said before, a phenomenon of nature. We know how to study nature, how to try to explain, at least provisionally, the physical living things of this world. We can ask, as we always have, how we are like, and how unlike, all the other creatures that just happen to be here as well. Is this not what all our science and all our poetry are for? What else is there to tell stories about?

Let us return again to the three primary questions.

To the question, "Where are we?" we must honestly reply that we do not have a clue, though we should also say that we have a persistent hunch that more is here than meets the eye.

Some would prefer to say that the world that we know is nothing more than big, dumb matter, spinning mute and gross, the outcome of aimless fire, not flawed, just all-consuming. But those who say that are no different than the rest of us. We know that they do not know if that is so. But if that is so, then we know that the world is not holy. And even if the universe is dumb and blind, it remains a hard, sure fact that we are creatures who have an idea of the holy.

All such musings lead us to the second primary question, and it becomes apparent that the only plausible initial response to the question, "Who are we?" is that we are the creature that does not know but tries to understand, the creature that suspects something is peculiar about the world and our presence in it, something in need of explaining.

Which leads to the third primary question, "What are we ex pected to do?" and so, to respond to the question, we consider the phenomenon. That is called a naturalistic ethic.

We were meant to do many things in many different ways. We were intended to consider eternity and the extent of the cosmos and how life works and is possible at all. We have a sense of space, by which we can probe outward indefinitely until we hit a limit that can define our whereabouts. We have a sense of depth that we can push backward to create a history, which can help us try to fathom how things came to be as they are.

We were designed to build snares and traps, to chisel stone, and later, when we had unlocked the codes of the elements, sili- con chips and beta blockers. We know how to make inferences between cause and effect and to visualize, step by step, how a plan of action might unfold and what accidents might make it go awry.

We teach the children right from wrong, the complexities of good manners and common caring, knowing all the while in humility that we do not understand or follow much about this.

We are able to play, to invent games of great complexity, simply to while away time, for the adventure of it. We are, of all things, funny, perhaps the strangest trait of all.

We watched the birds and learned to fly. We figured out, some- how, how to make hot from cold and cold from hot. We make art, we decorate, just for the love of it. We make up stories and theo- ries, histories, and step-by-step instructions, manuals, inventories, catalogues of tools.

We know how to promise, and we know the meanings of words like *betrayal, deceit,* and *dishonor.* We tell time. We predict eclipses. And much, much more.

EVOLUTION

And we were meant to try to account for our presence on this planet. This seems to amount to a choice between Genesis and

Darwin. These are the main creation myths of our culture. Darwin is by far the more fantastic and unfathomable.

We have strong evidence that over a period of about 4.3 billion years, life emerged and became more complex and abundant. It seems clear that Darwin was right about at least one thing. We had a common ancestor. As the late physician-essayist Lewis Thomas once charmingly put it, we all come down from a long line of cells. The story of evolution is a stunning one, and many of the most stunning parts have come to be known quite recently, the product of cosmological, paleobiological, and microbiological research in the past half century. We are still reeling from the news.

Perhaps we can agree that we must tell the young the story of evolution. But that is not the end of it. For the tale of evolution is no longer, if it ever was, a clear, straightforward, certified teaching. Rather, the more we have learned, the more dumbfounded we have become. So now we have to decide what story about evolution we are going to tell.

Let us return to a subject that we considered some time ago, the question of how our view of evolution affects our sense of meaning in the universe. The orthodox neo-Darwinian position is that life evolved gradually through a continual process of random mutation and natural selection according to Mendelian laws of inheritance. This has always been a stunning conception, a remarkable feat of human thought, and in many quarters it is still embraced dogmatically. Many teach that neo-Darwinian evolution is demonstrated truth. That is not the case. For many, through all the last century and a half, this version of the story has always lacked sheer credibility. In our time the uneasiness has increased.

Leave aside all the long-standing problems of gaps in the fossil record and the absence of pivotal intermediate forms. Do not worry here about the Cambrian explosion, the remarkable proliferation of new species that appears suddenly, perhaps as recently as ten million years ago, and simply does not square with Darwinian gradualism. Rather, the more interesting objections to Darwinian fundamentalism come from simple acts of contemplation of the sheer implausibility of the standard view.

In the late 1950s the chemist Stanley Miller and others initiated certain experiments simulating the creation of life in the primeval ooze. They combined hydrogen, ammonia, and methane, bombarded it with electrical shocks simulating lightning. After a while a brown stain of amino acids appeared. The scientists assumed that gradually more complex self-replicating molecules would evolve.

But functional proteins are extremely complex. Every link has to be just right, and the number of wrong possibilities is almost infinite. The chance that such a molecule could evolve by random mutation seems wildly incredible. Many early life biologists find it far more sensible to think not that amino acids evolved into DNA but that the process worked from DNA down, that DNA came first, imprinting the protein. But that implies that DNA emerged simply by chance in Darwin's warm pond.

There is more, of course, including the problem of species diversity. If life had emerged through a process of chance events, we would expect a broader spectrum of life forms, covering the array of logical possibilities. But for all their abundance and differentiation, species conform to a small number of basic forms: the streamlined fishes, the feathered birds, the insects, the mammals.

A simple contemplation of creatures makes the standard Darwinian view puzzling. Rather than random mutation, it seems more as though evolution had developed a set of prefabricated parts and recombined them in all sorts of ways. The eye of the octopus and the eye of the human are very much the same, though they emerge from different cellular structures. The jaw and the mandible are used, time and time again, across unrelated species.

The biologist Michael Behe asks us to imagine the evolution of the cilium, the tail by which some cells swim.[1] The cilium works roughly like a rotary engine. The tail spins in a circular well, powered by a chemical reaction. Consider now how a bicycle might mutate into a motorcycle. Something like a cylinder appears at the front sprocket. A protopiston emerges behind the seat. Then what is supposed to happen?

Those who subscribe to the anthropic principle hold that the conditions required for the creation of chemicals necessary for the evolution of life anywhere in the universe are exceedingly narrow. These were in fact the physical parameters of the emergence of the cosmos. For those who subscribe to this view, it looks like the universe was programmed for the creation of life.

In light of all this a surprisingly substantial number of scientists today are willing to say that it seems just as good a hypothesis to say that life is the product of intelligent design as that it emerged by blind chance and natural selection. On the whole, those who advance these views speak cautiously and diffidently. They do not elaborate on the story. They do not try to make a religious point. They simply say, in wonder and perplexity, that it seems highly unlikely that all this is just accident.

We could indeed tell other stories about evolution. Some years ago the Jesuit paleontologist Pierre Teilhard de Chardin argued that a pattern of increasing complexity is discernible in evolution, from atomic dust to intricate organisms to the emergence of mind, and from these, perhaps, to the unification of mind and spirit and the material world and thus to the realization of the human quest for understanding and unity and the fulfillment of the Christian hope.[2]

What do we intend to teach the next generation about all this? I think that things have gone too far for us just to endorse Darwinian orthodoxy and ignore the challenges. Nor do I think that we are right to continue to represent this as a dogmatic battle between literal Darwinists and literal creationists.

I think that we have to tell young people how grandly baffled we have become, how all our remarkable recent discoveries have left the world not more comprehensible but more dumbfounding. You may still, if you wish, imagine life emerging accidentally, aimlessly, in some tiny puddle. Or you can see—and there is no way I can soften the effect of the image—the hand of the designer fashioning the chemistry of life. Either view is utterly fantastic. We cannot say that one view is more scientifically accurate than the other. No other possibilities exist. And that, for the time being, is simply how matters stand.

Beyond life itself what story do we intend to tell about the evolution of humanity? We are here, so we must have been an evolutionary success. So scientific speculation, taking account of our qualities, tries to tell a plausible tale of why we were fitted to succeed.

Today, not surprisingly given the fixations of the age, many try to reduce the explanation to reproductive success. Who we are, these particular people who were destined to prevail, depends on who got to spread their sperm around most plentifully. So the learned now debate, solemnly if inconclusively, whether the cheaters, those most given to adultery, or the faithful, who women might more prize, would be more likely to pass more genes along.

Sociobiologists may debate whether aggression or altruism has fitted us for survival, but they remain obsessed, as evolutionists have for more than a century, with the question of the survival of the fittest. Nonetheless, as the evolutionary biologist Konrad Lorenz once observed, not all traits that are selected for lead to species success. Many will eventually drive a species to extinction.[3] We do not know, we cannot even guess in this reductionistic effort, which human qualities might in the end prove lethal to our kind.

The question of competitive selection, as we understand it, may tell us little about how we came to be as we are. After all, as the paleontologist Loren Eiseley saw, the first new creatures that carry the evolutionary process forward often seem more like failures than successes. "The first land fish was ... an incredibly ungainly and inefficient vertebrate.... He was a water failure who had managed to climb ashore."[4] The wet fish gasping for air hardly prevailed over competitors. A creature driven to the wall, by some fortune it had simply escaped.

We try to explain our human traits as the product of competitive selection. Our intelligence, we say, was highly selected by conquest and war. The parental instincts are simply necessary to care for our young in their long helplessness.

But none of this accounts for our capacity to think and wonder, to ponder our being and our meaning, traits clearly distinctive of humans, though their survival value is unreadable. Efforts to explain, as a matter of natural selection, the near universality of religion and worship among humans (as general as the incest taboo) are remarkably awkward and unpersuasive.[5]

But Eiseley imagines that those who by fluke dreamed and wondered sat by the fire with the hunters and the warriors, and they communicated their thoughts, and we began to think together. We became not just the products of natural selection but a social animal. We learned to make ourselves.

The natural process led not to selection for one human type but for many. We are distinctive not for specific traits on which survival might have rested but for the strange variety of capacities by which we enriched and complemented one another.

And Eiseley continues, among those around the campfire:

> Some of them, a mere handful in any generation perhaps, loved—
> they loved the animals about them, the soft song of the wind, the
> soft voices of women. On the flat surfaces of cave walls the three
> dimensions of the outside world took animal shape and form.
> Here—not with the ax not with the bow—man fumbled at the door
> of his true kingdom. Here, hidden in times of trouble behind silent
> brows, against the man with the flint, waits St. Francis of the
> birds—the lovers, the men who are still forced to walk warily
> among their own kind.[6]

THEORY

We are the creatures who try to comprehend, to make sense of our world and our place in it. We would do well to bear in mind the danger in this effort.

For us to understand, we must see pattern and relationship, a model of development, a history. We must subsume particulars under generalities, make categories, and draw distinctions. We must have a theory.

Nature does not mind our doing this. It humors us. Nature does not give a whit if we call that animal a raccoon or a fern a sporophyte. It is indifferent to our musings about atomic structure. Nature does not care whether we get it right.

It is otherwise when we try to understand people, which is our principal business. Here, how we impute motive, read character, or attribute cause to action matters greatly. We are playing with primeval fire. And our efforts usually are extraordinarily clumsy.

As I have said, to understand the others we must proceed hypothetically, by hunch and guesswork. We try out a motive or a meaning and try to judge by the response whether we have read what is in another mind. If we are wrong, we apologize, inquire further, and try again.

But this instinct built deep within us, this need to figure out the meaning and significance of our kind, has a perilous side. For the problem with our irresistible urge to understand is that we want to understand completely. Anomaly, puzzlement, contradiction rankle us to our depths. Every impulse that marks us as human impels us to try to overcome uncertainty. And yet we have been warned. That inescapable urge to know truly is the source of our sin. It is the subject of our oldest myth, the story of the garden.

The problem with our urge for comprehension is that it is inevitably reductionistic. We see pattern among a few phenomena of the world and, leaving the rest in darkness, presume that what adds up for us represents the truth about the whole. We have examined the consequences of material reductionism in science, how the decision to think only about the material stuff of the universe raised some patterns to dogma and excluded others. We have seen how we can reduce humanity to system by thinking of reason only as calculation or the self as only a social construct. We have seen how thinking of ourselves only in terms of evolutionary reproductive fitness creates a caricature of our nature.

We have to create categories if we are to organize our lives and be useful to one another. We may want to define *depression, neurosis,* and *denial* for therapeutic reasons so long as we do not then assume that we have thereby captured the meaning of all our sorrow. We may define people as intelligent or artistic or good at spatial relations, so long as we bear in mind that to classify people in such ways is not to understand them. All our categories touch people at just one point on the circle of their being. The rest remains unfathomable, unless we also, in love, through inquiry, try to establish a real relationship.

Those who feel that they have begun to comprehend humanity,

that they have a valid social theory, face insidious dangers. For to say that we understand another because that person fits a plot on the map of our theory, to insist that her interpretation of herself is not her but that she is, in truth, what our theory says, is to subordinate her, to reduce her to an artifact, perhaps an instrument, of our thought and of our will. The only remedy is to remain aware of the mystery of the other, her distance, his strangeness. And then we will comprehend ourselves again, the dark incompleteness of our longing, the obvious impossibility that we can comprehend ourselves, each other, and the meaning of our situation here.

The true terror is when the state tries to define a theory of humanity and make it mandatory. This is the politics of which we learned much in the century just past, the step beyond tyranny into the totalitarianism that so recently defined much of the world. And sadly, this was just a gross perversion of the yearning that makes us human, our helpless insistent desire to understand.

The last sentence I would have spoken in any course in the universities, the last sentence I would have written in any book about humanity is this: "In the end we will never understand fully. We were meant to live in mystery."

FAITH

Let me sum up. This is what I think the elders of a liberal democratic nation should teach each new generation.

I believe that we must teach them the lore, the language, the skills, and the folkways. We must teach them to be polite and responsible. We must teach them table manners, arriving on time, and cleaning up after themselves. I do not believe that an education in decency and self-discipline is incompatible with an education for freedom.

Beyond this I believe that we have the duty to teach them to be free in the serious sense of the word. Again, we must not teach them that freedom implies simply that they may do as they please. Nor shall we teach them simply to adapt, comply, and conform. Rather, we will teach them that they can be free if they use their powers to consider our teachings, interpret them, try to bring them closer to the ideals of justice and truth.

I think we must teach them to become awake and aware, conscious of their particularity, their uniqueness as a person, and thus that they must fashion a philosophy, a vocation, and a way that fits the unique individual that curiously and inexplicably they are.

I think we must teach them that it is not just their duty but their nature and their love to seek out the others, in all the ways and at all the levels that arise from care and inquiry, mutual exploration and discovery, the common endeavors of work and democracy.

I am sure that we must teach them to mistrust their first intuitions and reasons, for their ideas of the good are vague and uncertain, and many would seek to deceive them. They must learn to check out their judgments with the serious ones, the ones who intend to live in truth. These they must seek out and find, but there are more of them than the cynical believe.

We should help them become aware of their curious sense of the incompleteness of the world, and their cognizance of their own imperfection and finitude, for this is how they can come to know their place in the nature of things and their capacity for good and evil.

And this is as far as our common teaching should go. Beyond this lies the realm of faith.

The whole purpose of the public philosophy of liberal democracy is to open the possibility of faith. This sounds strange. We think of liberal democracy and religion as somehow antagonistic. But this has never really been the case. The whole purpose of liberal freedom is to open the individual to reason, inquiry, and wonder. And this is the starting point, the first condition, for any real development of faith. Liberal democracy is hostile to the inculcation of faith as dogma. But that is not faith at all. It does not arise out of wonder. It is simply an expression of obedience, of conformity to the world.

A free individual, I have said, aware of her own uniqueness and the strangeness of the world, knows that she must think by guesswork. To find another we must probe in shadows. The same is true if we try to understand the nature of the world, for nature likes to keep its secrets. We proceed hypothetically, according to our shrewdest hunches at the moment, and we revise and correct, abandon and start over, depending on how things turn out, whether the other responds, whether the world makes greater sense. To proceed in this way is technically called *pragmatism*. It is also the way of faith. To proceed in faith is to proceed on the basis of belief, not knowledge, conjecture, not certainty. To proceed in faith is to go beyond the established and the familiar in the hope of an understanding that will in fact come closer to the nature of the case, to truth or beauty or justice.

We can teach some things with great assurance. We can teach that part of the nature of our humanity is that we must make up a meaning for our presence here. We are not given that meaning, as are other creatures. That is why, in a free society, at precisely this point we must stay our hand. We cannot prescribe a story of our meaning for we do not know it. All we can do is open the door to faith. And we must tell the young that they cannot live without meaning. They were born for faith.

A free society is rich in the materials of faith. It contains all the possibilities in our legacy of philosophy, religion, science, literature, and art. The free society is a pluralistic society, but pluralism today has come to have two incompatible meanings. Some speak of a pluralism of mutually uncomprehending and suspiciously sullen groups, each protecting and nurturing its exclusive doctrine, united only by a crabbed liberalism of leaving one another alone. This is not the pluralism of freedom or of faith. That, instead, is a rich pluralism, a pluralism of abundance. It is a pluralism that contains all the possibilities of our imagination, our evidence, and our worship. That pluralism is open to everyone.

Some will find this idea unsettling. Many elders, we know, would insist that the young sustain their distinctive ways, the ways that set them apart. But the commitment of a free society clearly must be to enable the young to leave as well as to stay. Some will object that such a liberalism is not impartial among different valued ways of life. But liberalism has never been impartial. It is a defiant creed.

What do we hope will emerge from such teaching? Some of the young will, indeed, sustain the ways of the elders, but they will do so self-consciously. Others will embrace a creed with a passion—religion, chemistry—and make it their vocation and their way. Others will fashion a vision of their own, eclectic and personal, from the materials at hand. A few will see something startling and new as they contemplate their legacy, and they will lead us further down the path that we were intended to travel.

The way of faith is necessarily diverse and personal. Yet the discovery of faith is a common undertaking. Indeed, we must never enforce faith, for that destroys it. But the elders must not be reluctant to teach their own faith, their own vision. Indeed, they must teach what they believe with passion, with clarity and conviction, for the young must know this if they are to find a meaning of their own. In the end we live to pass meaning along.

Faith is precisely that. It is hope against darkness. It is understanding that knows itself to be incomplete. It is at once a conviction that we can know, however dimly and uncertainly, and it is an admission that we will never really understand. To be aware is to know that we were meant to live in mystery.

NOTES
INDEX

NOTES

CHAPTER 2. THE AWAKENING AND THE MEANING OF IT ALL

1. Karl Jaspers calls this the "axial period." See Jaspers, *The Origin and Goal of History*, trans. Michael Bullock (New Haven, Conn.: Yale University Press, 1953).

2. Martin Luther, "Luther at the Diet of Worms," in Luther, *Works*, ed. Helmut T. Lehmann (Philadelphia: Muhlenberg, 1958), 32:112–13.

CHAPTER 3. LIVING PHILOSOPHICALLY AND LIVING WELL

1. John Rawls, *A Theory of Justice* (Cambridge, Mass.: Harvard University Press, 1971), 409–10.

2. John Rawls, *Political Liberalism* (New York: Columbia University Press, 1993); Richard Rorty, *Contingency, Irony, and Solidarity* (New York: Cambridge University Press, 1989).

3. For an absolutely superb essay on Friedrich Wilhelm Nietzsche and Plato see Catherine Zuckert, *Postmodern Platos* (Chicago: University of Chicago Press, 1996), 10–32.

4. William James Booth, *Households* (Ithaca, N.Y.: Cornell University Press, 1993).

5. Charles Sanders Peirce, "The Fixation of Belief," in Peirce, *The Philosophical Writings of Peirce,* ed. Justus Buchler (New York: Dover, 1955), 5–22.

CHAPTER 4. WHAT IS FREEDOM FOR?

1. Michael Young, *The Rise of the Meritocracy* (Baltimore, Md.: Penguin, 1961), 108.

2. Thomas Hobbes, *Leviathan,* ed. Michael Oakeshott (New York: Collier, 1962).

3. Nancy Rosenblum, *Another Liberalism: Romanticism and the Reconstruction of Liberal Thought* (Cambridge, Mass.: Harvard University Press, 1987), 2.

4. Philip Selznick, *The Moral Commonwealth* (Berkeley: University of California Press, 1993), 388–91.

5. Michel Foucault, *Madness and Civilization* (New York: Random House, 1965); *Discipline and Punish* (New York: Pantheon, 1977); *The History of Sexuality* (New York: Vintage, 1980). I particularly like the discussion in William E. Connolly, *Politics and Ambiguity* (Madison: University of Wisconsin Press, 1987), 99–115.

6. Richard Rorty applauds Whitman's view of America as robust self-creation (*Achieving Our Country* [Cambridge, Mass.: Harvard University Press, 1998], 3–38). William Connolly would promote discord and ambiguity rather than reason and identity (*Politics and Ambiguity*). Richard Flathman speaks of "willful" liberalism (*Willful Liberalism* [Ithaca, N.Y.: Cornell University Press, 1992]).

CHAPTER 5. INDIVIDUALS AND THE POWERS WITHIN

1. Charles Taylor calls this the distinctly modern notion of morality that has roots in the eighteenth century (*The Ethics of Authenticity* [Cambridge, Mass.: Harvard University Press, 1991], 22–26). But I believe it has longer, more significant precedents.

2. See the variety of conceptions of autonomy in John Churchman, ed., *The Inner Citadel: Essays on Individual Autonomy* (New York: Oxford University Press, 1989).

3. Alasdair MacIntyre, *After Virtue* (South Bend, Ind.: University of Notre Dame Press, 1981), 32.

4. George Herbert Mead, *Mind, Self, and Society* (Chicago: University of Chicago Press, 1934).

5. Thomas Merton, *Contemplative Prayer* (New York: Doubleday, 1969).

6. Edmund Kahn, *The Sense of Injustice* (Bloomington: Indiana University Press, 1975).

7. Arthur Koestler, *The Ghost in the Machine* (London: Pan, 1967).

8. Immanuel Kant, *Groundwork of the Metaphysics of Morals*, trans. H. J. Paton (New Haven, Conn.: Yale University Press, 1964).

9. MacIntyre, *After Virtue*, 44.

10. Philip Selznick, *Law, Society, and Industrial Justice* (New York: Russell Sage, 1969).

11. John Rawls, *A Theory of Justice* (Cambridge, Mass.: Harvard University Press, 1971), 507–11.

12. MacIntyre, *After Virtue*, 1–5.

13. Thomas A. Spragens Jr., "The Antimonies of Social Justice," *Review of Politics* 55 (spring 1993): 193–217.

CHAPTER 6. ON HUMAN FRAILTY AND THE PROBLEM OF EVIL

1. Stephen C. Meyer, "The Methodological Equivalence of Design and Descent," in J. P. Moreland, ed., *The Creation Hypothesis* (Downers Grove, Ill.: InterVarsity Press, 1994), 67–112.

2. Ibid., 190–91.

3. Stephen Holmes, *The Anatomy of Antiliberalism* (Cambridge, Mass.: Harvard University Press, 1993).

4. Reinhold Niebuhr, *The Children of Light and the Children of Darkness* (New York: Scribner's, 1944).

5. This is what John Rawls calls the minimum condition of political liberalism; see his *Political Liberalism* (New York: Columbia University Press, 1993). It is also what Václav Havel calls "living in truth"; see his *Summer Meditations* (New York: Random House, 1993), 1–20.

6. The classic treatment of positivist moral emotivism is A. J. Ayer, *Language, Truth, and Logic* (New York: Doubleday, 1959). See also MacIntyre, *After Virtue* (South Bend, Ind.: University of Notre Dame Press, 1981), 11–33.

7. A wonderful series of essays on this theme from Charles Sanders Peirce appears in Susan Haack, *Manifesto of a Passionate Moderate* (Chicago: University of Chicago Press, 1999).

CHAPTER 7. INDIVIDUALITY AND RELATIONSHIP

1. I take this thought from Paul Tillich, *The Eternal Now* (New York: Scribner's, 1957), 147.

2. Martin Buber, *I and Thou* (New York: Scribner's, 1958).

3. Jean-Jacques Rousseau, "A Discourse on the Arts and Sciences" in Rousseau, *The Social Contract and Discourses*, ed. and trans. G. D. H. Cole (New York: Dutton, 1950), 148–49. For a nice commentary see Greg Hill, "The Politics of Transparent and Opaque Communities," *Polity* 29 (fall 1996): 1–26.

4. Will Kymlicka, *Liberalism, Community, and Culture* (Oxford: Clarendon, 1989), 47–53.

CHAPTER 8. TEACHING AND LEARNING

1. Pascal Boyer, *The Naturalness of Religious Ideas* (New York: Cambridge University Press, 1993).

2. Wayne Booth, *For the Love of It* (Chicago: University of Chicago Press, 1999).

3. Ludwig Wittgenstein, *Philosophical Investigations,* trans. G. E. M. Anscombe (New York: Macmillan, 1963), 59.

4. Noam Chomsky, *Cartesian Linguistics* (New York: Harper and Row, 1966).

5. For an interesting discussion of all this, see T. K. Seung, *Plato Reconsidered* (Lanham, Md.: Rowman and Littlefield, 1996), 291–319.

6. Stanley Cavell, *Conditions Handsome and Unhandsome* (Chicago: University of Chicago Press, 1990), xxxi.

CHAPTER 9. COMMUNITY

1. *Yoder v. Wisconsin,* 406 U.S. 205 (1972).

2. Michael Sandel, *Democracy's Discontent* (Cambridge, Mass.: Harvard University Press, 1996).

3. James Bernard Murphy, *The Moral Economy of Labor: Aristotelian Themes in Economic Theory* (New Haven, Conn.: Yale University Press, 1993), 8.

CHAPTER 10. WORKING RELATIONSHIPS

1. Gary Becker, *The Economic Approach to Human Behavior* (Chicago: University of Chicago Press, 1976).

2. Aristotle, *The Nichomachean Ethics* (Indianapolis, Ind.: Hackett, 1985), 28.

3. John Maynard Keynes, *The General Theory of Employment, Interest, and Money* (New York: Harcourt, Brace, 1964), chaps. 8–9.

4. Andrew Shonfield, *Modern Capitalism* (New York: Oxford University Press, 1965).

5. Neil J. Mitchell, *The Generous Corporation* (New Haven, Conn.: Yale University Press, 1989); Chester Barnard, *The Functions of the Executive* (Cambridge, Mass.: Harvard University Press, 1966).

6. William James Booth, *Households* (Ithaca, N.Y.: Cornell University Press, 1993).

7. Hannah Arendt, *The Human Condition* (New York: Doubleday, 1959).

8. Booth, *Households,* 2, 5.

9. James Bernard Murphy, *The Moral Economy of Labor: Aristotelian Themes in Economic Theory* (New Haven, Conn.: Yale University Press, 1993), 8.

10. Joseph Schumpeter, *A History of Economic Analysis* (New York: Oxford University Press, 1954), 53, 60.

11. Thorstein Veblen, *The Instinct for Workmanship* (New York: Norton, 1964).

12. Elizabeth Anderson, *Value in Ethics and Economics* (Cambridge, Mass.: Harvard University Press, 1993), 141–67.

13. Michael Walzer, *Spheres of Justice* (New York: Basic, 1983).

14. Harold Laski, *A Grammar of Politics* (London: George Allen and Unwin, 1973), 251.

15. Schumpeter, *History of Economic Analysis,* 131.

16. Thomas A. Spragens Jr., "The Antimonies of Social Justice," *Review of Politics* 55 (spring 1993): 193–217.

17. John Rawls, *A Theory of Justice* (Cambridge, Mass.: Harvard University Press, 1971), 507–11.

18. Ibid., 75–83.

CHAPTER 11. DEMOCRACY

1. Hannah Arendt, *The Human Condition* (New York: Doubleday, 1959).

2. Jürgen Habermas, *Moral Consciousness and Communicative Action,* trans. Christopher Lenhardt and Chierry Weber Nicholson (Cambridge, Mass.: MIT Press, 1990).

3. Karl Polanyi, *The Great Transformation* (Boston: Beacon, 1944).

CHAPTER 12. WHO DO WE THINK WE ARE?

1. Michael Behe, *Darwin's Black Box* (New York: Touchstone, 1996), 51–73.

2. Pierre Teilhard de Chardin, *The Phenomenon of Man* (New York: Harper, 1959).

3. Konrad Lorenz, *The Waning of Humaneness* (Boston: Little, Brown, 1983), 46–70.

4. Loren Eiseley, *The Star Thrower* (New York: Harcourt Brace, 1978), 18.

5. Walter Burkkert, *The Creation of the Sacred* (Cambridge, Mass.: Harvard University Press, 1996), 1–33.

6. Eiseley, *Star Thrower,* 307–8.

INDEX

Anderson, Elizabeth, 154
Arendt, Hannah, 152, 170
Aristotle, 7, 13–14, 16, 29, 31, 54, 64–67, 97, 128, 141, 149, 152, 153
Augustine, 7, 83
autonomy, 55–57, 104. *See also* freedom, individual; individuality

Behe, Michael, 189
Booth, William James, 152
Boyer, Pascal, 111

Cavell, Stanley, 131
Chomsky, Noam, 123
civility. *See* contract
community: and cultural conservatism, 51–53, 133–37; and economic enterprise, 155–59. *See also* inquiry; professions and professionalism
conservatism, cultural, 8, 51–53; and community, 23–25, 133–37; and evil, 79–80, 84; and individuality, 51–53, 95, 97–98
contract, 42–47; and relationships, 101–3. *See also* markets

democracy, theory of, 170–81; and civic education, 173–75; and living philosophically, 28–31, 179–81. *See also* liberal democracy
Democritus, 13
Dewey, John, 7, 20, 28, 54, 82

economics. *See* contract; markets; political economy; practical reason; utilitarianism
education. *See* teaching and learning
Eichmann, Adolph, 86
Eiseley, Loren, 191–92
entrepreneurship: and practical reason, 152–64
evil, human, 76–90; and conservatism, 79–80, 84; and liberal democracy, 79–84; and moral education, 173–75
evolution, 11–12, 77–78, 187–92

Foucault, Michael, 48–49
freedom, individual, 5–7, 35–53; and conservatism, 51–53; and living philosophically, 25–28; and love, 61–64; and postmodernism, 48–51; and practical reason,

206

64–67; and utilitarianism, 37–41.
See also individuality

Heraclitus, 13
Hobbes, Thomas, 15, 43–44
Hoyle, Frederick, 77
Human nature: images of, 9–10,
12–13, 36–37, 50–51, 69–70,
106–8, 185–97

idealism, philosophic, 3–17; liberal,
67–69. See also philosophy,
public
individuality, 17, 36–53, 69–72,
93–108; and civic education,
84–90; and community, 143–47;
and conservatism, 51–53; and
democracy, 28–31; and economic
organization, 152–64; and
justice, 164–69; and living
philosophically, 25–28 ; and
relationships, 93–108, 129–32;
and teaching and learning, 110,
127–32; and universality,
122–30. See also freedom,
individual; philosophy, public
inquiry, 10, 27–28, 120–22; and
community, 139, 143–47; and
democracy, 172; and individuality,
27–29, 95–98; and moral
education, 88–90; and political
economy, 152–64; and practical
reason, 64–69; and professions
and professionalism, 142–43;
and relationships, 96–97, 103–5

Kant, Immanuel, 7, 14, 15–16, 54,
57–61
Keynes, John Maynard, 149

liberal democracy: and democracy,
173–78; and evil, 79–84; as
public philosophy, 22, 36–53,

100, 118–22; and relationships,
179–81; and teaching and
learning, 110. See also freedom,
individual; philosophy, public
liberalism. See liberal democracy
Locke, John, 15, 42, 44–46, 53, 81,
100, 173
love (agapé), 61–64, 104
Luther, Martin, 17

MacIntyre, Alasdair, 66–67
markets: and equality and elitism,
159–62; and liberal democracy,
38–41, 130–31. See also contract;
political economy; utilitarianism
Marx, Karl, 20, 29, 41, 82, 152
Mead, George Herbert, 55
Miller, Stanley, 189
Murphy, James Bernard, 141, 152

Niebuhr, Reinhold, 80
Nietzsche, Friedrich, 9, 29, 49

Peirce, Charles Sanders, 7, 89
philosophy, public, 3–11, 18–21;
Greek, 13–14; and living
philosophically, 21–31 passim
Plato, 13–14, 15, 19, 28, 54, 64, 110,
123, 152, 153. See also Socrates
Polanyi, Karl, 175
political economy: and economic
organization, 149–64; and
justice, 164–69; and practical
reason, 152–64. See also
contract; markets; utilitarianism
postmodernism, 9, 48–51
practical reason, 7–9, 98–99, 104–8;
and democracy, 140–43, 173–75;
and individual freedom, 64–67;
and political economy, 152–64;
and teaching and learning, 140–43
professions and professionalism,
86–87, 96–97, 137–39, 152–64

property, right of, 45
Pythagoras, 13–14

rational practice. *See* practical reason
Rawls, John, 22, 60, 167
relationships. *See* community;
    conservatism, cultural;
    individuality; inquiry; liberal
    democracy; teaching and learning
Rosenblum, Nancy, 47
Rousseau, Jean-Jacques, 94–95

Sandel, Michael, 140
Schumpeter, Joseph, 153
science: and public philosophy, 16,
    118–22; and reductionism,
    77–78, 192–94
Selznick, Philip, 47, 59
social contract. *See* contract; Locke,
    John
Socrates, 15, 17. *See also* Plato
Socratic dialogue, 124–25

teaching and learning, 3–11, 109–32;
    and civic education, 140–43,
    173–75; and moral education,
    84–90; and practical reason,
    64–67, 140–43
Teilhard de Chardin, Pierre, 190
Thales, 13

universality, human, 99, 122–26
utilitarianism: as public philosophy,
    8–9, 14, 37–41. *See also* contract;
    markets; political economy

Veblen, Thorstein, 153–54
vocations and vias, 72–75, 162–64

Walzer, Michael, 154
Wittgenstein, Ludwig, 119

Yoder v. Wisconsin, 135

DATE DUE

GAYLORD | | | PRINTED IN U.S.A.